APPLICATIONS OF DIRECT COSTING

Research Report 37

National Association of Accountants

The Classics Series

NAA *Classics* are those Association publications that have stood up well in the test of time. Published originally more than 10 years ago, these reprints are still "best-sellers" in that readers' demand for them continues. The reason lies in their contents; certain accounting principles and practices do not change.

Research Report No. 37
January 1, 1961

CONTENTS

Foreword

Research report published by

National Association of Accountants
Founded 1919 as the National Association of Cost Accountants
10 Paragon Drive, Montvale, N.J. 07645

FOREWORD

The analysis of cost-volume-profit relationships has long been familiar to economists and it has often been implicit in the patterns of thinking employed by business management in making decisions. Applications of this analysis appear to have been developed and described by a number of individuals working independently. The techniques and tools which resulted from this development were summarized in a series of N.A.A. research reports entitled *The Analysis of Cost-Volume-Profit Relationships* published during 1949-50.

A prior N.A.A. research study also disclosed a cost accounting system installed in 1908 which was designed to provide marginal cost data for pricing.[1] The earliest published description of such a cost system discovered in this prior study appeared in 1936. In this article the term "direct costing" was used for the first time to describe a system in which the marginal approach was employed both for accumulating costs in the accounts and for reporting periodic income.[2]

Growing interest in direct costing led N.A.A. to undertake a study of the subject and, in 1953, a research report entitled *Direct Costing* was published. While a substantial literature dealing with the subject had accumulated by that time, only a few companies using direct costing could be found when research underlying the report was done. Consequently, the report was primarily analytical.

Since 1953, interest in direct costing has spread widely. Evidence of this interest can be seen in the fact that, during 1959, N.A.A. held two subject conferences devoted exclusively to direct costing and on each occasion registrations had to be limited to the number of persons that could be accommodated by physical facilities available. In total, approximately 800 persons attended the two conferences. Direct costing has also been put to use by a growing number of companies and, by now, these companies have accumulated a substantial amount of experience with the

---

[1] *Direct Costing*, Research Series No. 23, 1953, p. 4.

[2] Jonathan N. Harris, "What Did We Earn Last Month?", *N.A.(C.)A. Bulletin*, Jan. 15, 1936.

1

method. The Research Planning Committee accordingly recommended a second study to ascertain how direct costing is being used currently.

This report summarizes the experience of fifty companies which participated in the study by contributing information about their applications of direct costing. In each case, a depth interview was employed to ascertain how direct costing is used, why the specific methods were chosen, and what results have been obtained. Field work continued until additional interviews no longer yielded new material. Interviews showed that a few of the companies visited had very limited experience with direct costing and, after these companies were excluded from the sample, fifty companies remained. In addition, members of the N.A.A. research staff attended subject and seminar conferences devoted to direct costing. Findings from the field study were checked against experiences of other companies represented at these conferences. Literature published since 1953 has also been drawn upon for material appearing in this report.

In some areas the study goes beyond the reporting of practice and endeavors to develop a logical foundation of reasoning to explain certain practices. This procedure follows from a recommendation by the Research Planning Committee that N.A.A. research studies should place more emphasis upon basic research to improve the understanding of accounting practice.

In general, management of companies participating in this study feel that its experience with direct costing has been favorable. This opinion and the reasons why it is held are reported in the pages which follow. However, they are findings from the field study and should not be interpreted as views advocated by N.A.A. because the Association does not issue judgments on accounting practices.

chapter 1

THE NATURE OF DIRECT COSTING

Appraisal of any costing method requires an understanding of the various uses which are made of cost data and the relationships among these uses. Present day accounting is concerned with past, present, and future costs. Past costs are matched with revenue by time periods to determine periodic income. Current costs are compared with planned costs (i.e., standards and budgets) to measure performance in controlling costs. Future costs are forecasted to provide management with data required for decision making and forward planning.

In addition to primary uses, each set of costs serves secondary uses which require that the whole costing structure be tied together in order that all needs may be met with relevant figures. Thus historical costs, while developed primarily for the purpose of matching costs and revenue to determine periodic income, have other uses. They provide the cost experience which is needed in forecasting future costs. And, when compared with previously forecasted costs for a period or project, they provide the opportunity for relating results to plans and forecasts. Consequently, both primary and secondary uses need to be considered in appraising any costing method.

Absorption Costing and the Matching Process

Early accounting systems for manufacturing enterprises recorded costs in accounts classified only by nature of expense— that is, as materials, wages, taxes, etc. For setting selling prices and costing periodic inventories, product costs were estimated. These estimating procedures developed into costing systems which were often independent of the financial accounts. However, the advantages of having the cost accounts tied in with the financial accounts were recognized at an early date.

In the beginning, cost accounting emphasized the application of historical costs to products as a part of the income determination process. The costing method developed for this purpose has

3

come to be known as *absorption costing*. It is based on the theory that all manufacturing costs, with the exception noted below, should be applied to the products manufactured and should follow the products through inventory to cost of goods sold. Under this theory, costs assigned to products sold during a period are matched with the revenue from sales of these products to determine gross margin. Costs assigned to products unsold in the period of production are deferred in inventory for matching in a later period. On the other hand, non-manufacturing costs are matched with revenue on a time basis by deducting the non-manufacturing costs incurred during a time period from the gross margin for that period.

In the application of this theory, the principal problems have centered around the assignment of indirect manufacturing costs to products. The direct costs of manufacturing can be traced to the products or jobs to which they apply, but indirect manufacturing costs, because they are indirect, can often be allocated only on the basis of assumed relationships between production and cost.

Moreover, it is necessary to choose the volume of production over which indirect costs are to be allocated. Since some indirect costs do not vary proportionately with the rate of activity, unit cost tends to fluctuate inversely with the volume chosen as a base for costing purposes. Selection of the volume base is an important but, in considerable measure, a subjective decision.

To allocate indirect costs on the basis of a predetermined volume (whether for the period in question or for a "normal" period) frequently results in under or over absorption of costs. This has created the problem of disposing of such over and under absorbed balances. Current practice seems to favor crediting overabsorbed balances of material amount to the products produced, i.e., to inventory and cost of goods sold, and treating underabsorbed balances as costs of the period.[3] Thus, the one exception to the theory that all manufacturing costs should be assigned to products is that underabsorbed manufacturing costs are excluded from product costs and charged in total to the period. In practice, absorption costing theory is often incompletely applied because various indirect manufacturing costs (e.g. depreciation, property taxes, insurance) are charged off currently instead of being applied to production and carried through inventory.

---

[3] See *Montgomery's Auditing*, 8 ed. (Ronald Press Co., New York, 1957), p. 198.

Influence of Other Uses for Costs

Over the years since absorption costing was developed for product costing and income measurement, the cost accounting function in business has been extended to include also the provision of data for cost control and planning. Increasing managerial concern with cost control led to standard costs, budgets, and responsibility accounting. At first the standard costs were kept separate from the accounts and, to the extent that accountants participated in comparing actual costs with standard costs, this was a task supplemental to their accounting duties. Eventually it was found that cost control could be strengthened and cost accounting procedures could often be facilitated by incorporating standard costs and responsibility classifications into the accounts. An important feature of these advances in the cost control function of accounting was modification of internal manufacturing cost and income statements to display standard cost of goods manufactured and variances from standard cost.

Since, under absorption costing theory, all manufacturing costs are charged to the products produced, there is no need to distinguish among these costs in costing products. On the other hand, actions to control costs must be taken before the costs are incurred and for this purpose management needs to know how much cost is allowable for the volume of production or rate of activity anticipated. Determination of allowable costs rests upon knowledge of the rate at which the amount of each cost changes with volume and other independent variables. Thus, with the development of standard costs and flexible budgets, the accountant learned to distinguish between costs which vary with production or sales volume and costs which tend to remain constant in amount while volume varies. The understanding of cost behavior derived from his cost control work improved the accountant's ability to forecast costs and aided him in the development of techniques to provide better costs for decision making, pricing, and profit planning.

As with the costing of products and the use of standard costs, the analysis of cost-volume-profit relationships to aid management in planning and decision making was first a subject for statistical studies carried on apart from the accounting processes of recording and reporting costs and income. This approach was necessary because, when absorption costing theory is followed in accounting for costs, both costs which vary with volume and costs which do not vary with volume are mixed together in the processes of accumulating and distributing costs.

5

However, accountants began to experiment with methods for integrating cost-volume-profit analysis techniques into the cost accounting process in order that the results might be made available to management in product cost statements and income reports. One company representative described direct costing as a cost system "which provides for the generation of actual figures rather than a statistical analysis of the variable and period elements of cost" and the earlier N.A.A. research report stated that "Direct costing applies to cost accounting statements the same principles of cost-volume-profit relationship which are illustrated by the break-even chart." Thus direct costing was developed as a method to make accounting for past costs consistent with accounting for present and future costs.

Direct Costing and the Matching Process

Direct costing, like absorption costing, is a method for matching costs with revenues to determine periodic income. Under absorption costing, manufacturing costs are assigned to products for matching with revenues in the period when revenues from sales of the products are recognized while other costs are matched with revenues in the same period in which the costs are incurred. Thus the basis for distinction is whether the costs were incurred for performance of a manufacturing or a non-manufacturing function.

On the other hand, under direct costing the distinction between direct cost and period cost determines when costs are matched with revenues. Direct costs are assigned to products and matched with revenues when revenues from the related products are recognized while period costs are matched with revenues in the period in which the costs are incurred.

Period costs of manufacturing arise from the provision of capacity for production and from keeping this capacity in readiness regardless of the extent to which it is utilized. Within the range of volume for which provision is made, period costs are neither increased in total by added production nor decreased by reduced production. Because the opportunity to use capacity expires with time, the costs of providing such capacity are also considered to expire with time.

Direct manufacturing costs are the additional costs incurred if goods are produced or the costs not incurred if goods are not produced. In total, direct costs tend to vary directly with volume of production. Within limited ranges of volume, this variation in cost also tends to be proportional to volume and hence unit cost tends to be constant in amount.

While, in the preceding two paragraphs, direct and period costs have been defined in terms of manufacturing, non-manufacturing costs are also direct or period in nature. For example, while most marketing costs are incurred to provide marketing capacity and are therefore period costs, commissions paid to salesmen are costs which arise only when goods are sold and the amount of commission cost tends to vary with sales volume.

The matching process is carried out under direct costing by first deducting from the revenue from products sold during a time period all of the direct costs of manufacturing and selling those products. The resulting balance, called *marginal income* or *contribution margin,* measures the contribution which the revenue for the period has made toward meeting the period costs of providing manufacturing and marketing capacity. Net income is then determined by deducting the period costs from marginal income.

Within the range of volume for which period costs remain constant, unit marginal income also tends to remain constant. This fact makes it possible to forecast the increment in net income which will result from any specified increment in volume, provided the marginal income rate is known.

Reported Net Income Under the Two Methods of Matching

When the inventory of manufactured goods fluctuates from period to period, absorption costing and direct costing give somewhat different net income figures. The reason for this difference is that absorption costing causes period costs to be deferred in inventory while direct costing defers no period costs. Thus in a month when inventory is increased, the net income reported by absorption costing will exceed the net income reported by direct costing because under absorption costing a portion of the month's period costs are charged to inventory while under direct costing the full amount of the month's period costs are charged against revenues of the month. When inventory is decreased, period costs which have been absorbed in inventory are liquidated with the result that the amount of period cost charged against revenues exceeds the amount incurred during the month. Hence a smaller net income will be reported by absorption costing than by direct costing. Only when the inventory of manufactured goods does not change dur-

7

ing the accounting period will net income reported by the two methods be identical. For any given period the difference between net income figures determined by absorption costing and by direct costing is equal to the change in the amount of period cost deferred in inventory.

Direct Costing in Historical Perspective

Viewed in historical perspective, it can be seen that cost accounting originated as a group of techniques for ascertaining product costs. Over the years, advances in management technology created needs for additional types of cost and income margin data. At first, these data were obtained by special studies and reported as statistics apart from financial statements prepared from the accounts. However, cost control and certain kinds of operating decisions are continuing problems and management's need for financial data relevant to these problems is recurring. Hence the service which cost accounting supplies to management was broadened by modifying accounting systems to accumulate the additional kinds of data and by designing accounting reports to communicate the information.

The integration of product costing with the financial accounts provided a means for checking product costs used for pricing and inventory costing; standard costs and responsibility accounting enabled the accountant to measure and report performance in controlling current costs; and direct costing provided through the accounting system data helpful in short-run profit planning and in making operating decisions. Thus direct costing is not a new or different kind of cost system, but is only a feature introduced into a process or job order cost system to broaden its usefulness. All of the fifty companies participating in this study use standard costs as well as direct costing.

Acceptance of Direct Costing

However, the extent to which direct costing is currently accepted varies widely. The four schools of thought described below can be distinguished among opinions expressed by accountants.

1. *The absorption costing school.* Members of this school feel that absorption costing provides a better measure of periodic income and a better inventory cost figure than does direct costing. To the extent that they recognize the need for different types of costs for cost control and cost planning, they prefer to develop these costs by analysis and special studies and see

8

no need to coordinate costs for different purposes within the accounting system.

2. *The modified absorption costing school.* Members of this group recognize the usefulness of direct and period costs for control and planning purposes and accumulate these classes of costs separately in the accounts in order that the desired cost data may be available without analysis. Flexible budgets and separate burden rates for direct and period components of manufacturing overhead are commonly used. However, in measuring periodic income those who hold this view follow absorption costing theory.

3. *The direct-costing-for-internal-use-only school.* Adherents to this point of view favor direct costing for internal management purposes including periodic income measurement, but feel that direct costing cannot or should not be used in external reporting. Where this opinion prevails, inventory and net income are determined on a direct costing basis and then adjusted to an absorption costing basis in those financial reports released to persons outside the management group.

4. *The direct costing school.* Members of this school favor the application of direct costing in financial reporting, external as well as internal.

The Test of Experience

It is apparent that each of these schools of thought has a somewhat different concept of just what direct costing is, what can be accomplished by its use, and how the accomplishment is brought about. Similar differences of opinion have long existed with respect to other cost accounting techniques such as standard costs, although these differences have tended to diminish with time. The present study was undertaken in the expectation that a survey of the experience of a number of companies which use direct costing would help to clarify many of the points on which there are differences of opinion. In reporting the findings in this study, separate chapters have been devoted to each of the major areas in which cost data are used. The first part of each chapter contains a discussion of the kinds of cost information which experience has shown are relevant for the intended use. This is followed by a description of practices found in the field study to illustrate applications of direct costing data in each of the areas considered and some of the variations which exist.

chapter 2

SEPARATION OF DIRECT
AND PERIOD COSTS

The usefulness of cost and income margin data derived from direct costing stems from the classification of costs into direct and period categories. For this reason, it is important to define carefully the terms direct cost and period cost. Moreover, it is essential to make sure that both accounting and managerial personnel concerned understand the application of these definitions in their company.

Definition of Terms

Period Cost

Period costs arise from keeping capacity to manufacture and to sell in readiness for use. In total, the cost of such capacity does not change with fluctuations in the volume of current activity so long as the amount of capacity remains the same. As described in the earlier N.A.A. research report on direct costing where the term "fixed cost" was used rather than period cost:[4]

> "Fixed costs are associated with facilities which are provided and kept in readiness without regard to the current actual volume of production and sales. Some of these facilities must be acquired and kept in a state of readiness more or less irrespective of the volume of orders on hand at the moment. Buildings, machines, and an organization comprising at least the key executive, technical, and supervisory personnel are examples of facilities which cannot be readily acquired or dispensed with in response to short period swings in volume. In addition, there are also fixed costs incurred because management has decided to make expenditures for advertising, sales promotion, employee training, and research without regard to current sales or production volume. Therefore, the significant characteristic of fixed costs is that their amount

---

[4] *Direct Costing*, Research Series No. 23, p. 12.

is related to the volume of business for which provision has been made rather than to the currently prevailing volume. For this reason the amount of the fixed costs is independent of current volume changes."

A closely similar concept is expressed in the following definition from one company's accounting manual:

"Period costs are those costs which would be required to manage, maintain, and develop the business whether or not specific products were actually made and sold."

After an extended search for a descriptive term acceptable to its executives, one company participating in this study chose "programmed indirect costs" to emphasize that the amount of such costs is determined by the operating program contained in the year's budget. Other terms reported in the field study are "capacity cost," "committed cost," and "readiness to serve cost."

Direct Cost

Usage of capacity to make and to sell goods or services requires that additional costs be incurred. Such costs of producing and selling tend to vary directly and proportionately with the volume of production or sales. For this reason, the term "variable cost" is often used as a synonym for direct cost. A typical definition of direct cost supplied by one of the companies participating in this study follows:

"Direct costs are those costs which vary directly with volume (raw material, direct labor, and direct supplies) plus certain costs which vary closely with production and can be allocated to a product or group of products on a reasonably accurate basis. This definition was chosen because it fills our need for clear-cut costs in analyzing results of operations and in making short run decisions on product pricing."

Costs are not inherently direct or period in nature, but acquire these characteristics as the result of managerial decisions with respect to organization and control of cost factors. For example, a decision to mechanize an operation usually entails a higher proportion of period costs than exists where the same operation is performed by hand. Likewise, a decision to retain certain employees regardless of volume creates a period cost while a decision to control the number of employees with volume of work to be done makes the same cost direct. In several companies it was found that the wages of all plant employees are classified as a period cost because it is a policy to maintain a steady labor force even though it may be necessary at times to assign productive workers to makeshift jobs.

11

Semivariable Costs

Some costs display characteristics of both direct and period costs. Hence they are called semivariable costs. One reason for this is that individual cost classifications often contain both direct and period components. For example, one company found that the cost of coal used to make steam for processing varied with production volume while the consumption of coal to make steam for heating and air conditioning was constant with time. Such costs can be analyzed into direct and period components.

Other costs vary irregularly with volume because production factors cannot be divided into infinitely small units. To illustrate, when additional volume is obtained by adding another shift, a complete set of supervisors, clerks, etc. must be added. When such costs are charted against volume, their movements appear as a series of steps rather than a continuous line. Practice in the classification of this type of cost is described later in this chapter.

Non-volume Cost Factors

There are many factors which may cause costs to vary. Clear thinking with respect to classification of costs on the basis of their response to volume (i.e., as direct or period costs) requires that the influence of factors other than volume be distinguished. For example, changes in prices paid for materials, in labor rates and labor efficiency, and production equipment all affect costs. However, such factors are distinguishable from cost changes attributable to varying volume by the fact that they would occur in the absence of any changes in volume.

In order to measure the effect of volume apart from the effects of other cost influencing factors such as purchase price of materials, labor efficiency, etc., it is necessary to hold the non-volume factors constant. This is accomplished by setting standards for the other factors and by observing the changes in cost which accompany changes in volume while other independent variables are charged to production at standard cost. In practice, variances will always arise and these variances are not completely independent of volume.[5] Nevertheless, the reaction of cost to changing volume can be measured precisely enough to be useful.

---

[5] For example, materials price variance may be, in part, the result of purchasing a quantity larger or smaller than that for which the standard price was set.

Conditions Affecting Classification of Costs into Direct and Period Categories

The response of costs to volume changes is affected by circumstances which vary from company to company and from time to time within a given company. For this reason, the classification of individual items of cost as direct or period cost is not uniform among the companies participating in this study or even within some individual companies. Moreover, experience of companies that have used direct costing over a period of years usually shows that some costs are shifted from one category to another to conform to changing conditions.

The principal circumstances which underlie differences in the classification of costs as direct or period are:

1. Differences in units used to measure increments in volume.
2. Differences in purposes for which costs are used.
3. Differences in the degree of precision desired in separation of direct and period costs.

Discussion and illustration of these differences follows.

Unit Used to Measure Increments in Volume

If an increment in output is defined as a single product unit, the amount of cost added by its production (or saved by not producing it) usually consists of direct material and labor plus a comparatively limited amount of variable manufacturing expense. As successively larger increments in production are contemplated, the amount of additional expense traceable to the added production tends to increase. In general, direct cost becomes more inclusive as the unit of output being costed increases in size relative to the total production of the company.

Moreover, the amount of period cost remains constant only within the range of volume normally experienced. If volume increases beyond this range, management usually decides to expand capacity and thereby to increase period cost. Conversely, when volume drops below the normal range, management may take action to reduce the period costs. In the short-run, personnel and purchased services are cut and, if the lower volume is expected to continue, excess plant and equipment are disposed of.

The volume unit used for measuring direct cost changes with the nature and scope of the decisions being made. Since a majority of the companies participating in this study have adopted direct costing for its usefulness in short-range profit planning, the unit of output chosen is one relevant to such decisions. Profit planning of this type is usually concerned with evaluating the contribution to profit made by comparatively small increments in total volume. Ordinarily these increments represent individual orders, customers, the sales increases attributable to sales promotion proposals, and similar limited segments of total sales. In dealing with such segments, most companies define direct costs as costs which vary directly in amount with the unit in which sales of production is customarily measured.

Period cost is defined to include all costs not directly variable with the unit chosen for measuring volume of production. For example, one company classifies payroll taxes as period cost. While the total payroll tax varies with changes in payroll, these variations have been found to be unrelated to standard productive hours allowed, which is the unit used for measuring factory production. Only costs varying with standard productive hours are classified as direct. Further, two other companies treat all fringe benefits as period costs because it is more convenient to handle them this way and the practice is thought not to distort the operating picture to a material extent. Similar explanations were given by those companies which classify payroll taxes, group insurance, and workman's compensation applicable to direct workers as direct costs whereas vacation wages, holiday pay, and pension costs are classed as period costs.

Purposes for Which Costs Are Used

As stated above, a majority of the companies participating in this study have designed their direct costing plans primarily to supply cost and income margin data for profit planning and for making current operating decisions. However, in some companies cost control has received major emphasis and in a few cases direct costing is used principally for costing inventory. Practice in the classification of costs—particularly borderline and semi-variable items—as direct or period costs is influenced by the principal purpose for which direct costing is used in each case.

Where profit planning objectives predominate, borderline items are usually put into the direct category to make sure that management is not led to make an unprofitable decision by the understatement of direct cost. The following examples illustrate this practice:

    1. This company frequently accepts individual orders at prices below full cost to make and sell the products. If there is any

question about the variability of a cost item, it is put into the direct cost classification to make sure that orders are not accepted at a price below direct cost. Thus all indirect labor is classified as direct cost even though some of it is semivariable or fixed.

2. Management frequently asks questions such as:

> How much does a given product or department contribute to period cost and profit?

> How much could be saved by eliminating a department or process?

> What contribution would be made by a proposed new product at various selling prices under consideration?

In order to answer these questions, the company includes in direct cost all items which would be eliminated if the product or department were discontinued. Included are supervision and, in those cases where existing equipment would have no other use, depreciation on this equipment is also included in direct cost.

3. Experience showed that monthly machine maintenance cost tended to fluctuate inversely with volume because, whenever possible, maintenance work was deferred until equipment was not needed for production. Machine maintenance costs are reasonably variable when compared to production on a yearly basis, but not from month to month. Since the company's products are sold in a strongly competitive market, management wants reliable contribution margin figures as a guide in deciding whether to accept or reject business. Consequently, maintenance is classified as a direct cost to make sure that marginal income is not overstated. To level the expense, each operating department receives a monthly charge based upon pounds produced, machine running time, or some other factor and the offsetting amount is credited to a maintenance reserve account. The actual expenses are then charged against the latter which, at the end of the year, usually comes fairly close to balancing out.

On the other hand, emphasis upon cost control usually leads to exclusion from direct cost of any items not fully controllable by departmental supervisors. Certain items excluded for this reason are, to some extent, variable with production volume. Illustrations from the field study follow:

4. Semivariable costs are classified as direct or period costs according to whether they are controlled with current production volume or budgeted as monthly amounts independent of short-run volume fluctuations. For example, wages of millwrights assigned to individual departments are budgeted as fixed costs per month but wages of millwrights assigned to a service pool are budgeted as direct cost because the usage of such services is controlled with production. Fringe benefit

15

costs follow the classification of related employees' wages because they are controlled with wages of the individuals. Any change in method of control from fixed to variable cost or vice-versa brings a corresponding change in classification as direct or period cost.

Changes in the assignment of responsibility for control may lead to changes in classification of costs. For example, fringe costs were first classified as period cost because these costs were viewed as a responsibility of the personnel department. Management now views fringe benefits as a part of wages which is a production responsibility. Hence fringe benefit costs are now classified as direct cost.

In contrast, management's desire to provide an incentive to control certain items with volume sometimes leads to their inclusion with direct costs even though these items are not wholly variable with production. An example of such an expense might be material handling performed by a central trucking department.

Where direct costing has been in use for an extended period of time, changes in the major problems facing management have usually led to change in the classification of some costs as direct or period. These changes in classification have been made to provide cost and income margin data relevant to decisions being made at the time. An illustration follows:

5. When this company first adopted direct costing approximately ten years ago, management was desirous of improving its control over costs. For this reason, direct costs were defined as those costs which could be controlled by first line supervisors with short-period swings in volume. In addition, the company had considerable unused capacity and management took a short-range point of view in determining what fixed costs could be left out of consideration in bidding for special orders to increase volume.

At the present time, management feels that costs are well controlled. Over the years, excess plant capacity has been absorbed by growth in volume of sales and management is now concerned with finding the most profitable uses for a limited amount of production capacity. Where it formerly wanted costs to guide decisions on low priced orders, it now wants costs to aid in selecting the most profitable products. Since this involves addition or subtraction of the entire output of products and departments, period costs are now more broadly defined to include all costs affected by such decisions.

Use of costs for profit planning leads to analysis of non-manufacturing costs as well as manufacturing costs into direct and period components. Such analysis of non-manufacturing costs is, of course, unnecessary for costing inventory. While costs of marketing, research, and administration are largely planned and controlled as period costs, items of cost which are variable with volume may exist, particularly among selling costs. However, the manner in which selling operations are organized and controlled determines whether or not individual cost items are direct or period charges. For example, salesmen's compensation is a period cost if salesmen are paid on a salaried basis and it is a direct cost if salesmen are paid on a commission basis. Order filling costs such as shipping and transportation may contain variable components.

Coordination of Uses

Costs are, of course, wanted for a variety of purposes and this fact raises the question of coordinating different definitions of direct and period cost relevant to the several purposes. In applying direct costing, the definitions incorporated into the accounts are framed to give costs of the type relevant to questions which recur frequently. In the words of one company representative:

> "Classification of costs, to be useful, must be related to the major purposes for which direct costing has been adopted. In this company, these purposes require that classification of costs as direct or period should be made on the basis of cost behavior over a maximum period of one month."

Thus, a majority of the companies participating in the study have adopted direct costing primarily for short-range profit planning and definitions of direct and period cost used in accounting for costs are stated with this purpose in view. Historical product cost and product income margin data for profit planning can therefore be drawn from the accounts and estimates can later be compared with actual figures recorded in the accounts.

However, in every company there are occasions for which direct and period costs need to be defined and calculated somewhat differently. For occasions which arise infrequently, costs are best prepared by special study. For example, if a question such as whether or not to replace a machine arises, period costs related to the existing machine will be eliminated and new period costs added if the replacement is made. Machine operating costs taken from the accounts therefore need to be adjusted to reflect alternatives in the decision. In general, any decision involving unusually large changes in volume, addition or elimination of products, changes in plant and equipment, or major alterations in the company's advertising or research program are likely to

17

affect period costs and perhaps also direct costs. Preparation of cost analyses relevant to such decisions often begins with cost data taken from the accounts.

Precision in Separation of Direct and Period Costs

Since high precision in cost classification usually increases accounting expense, the degree of precision sought in separating direct and period costs should be commensurate with the resulting benefits. If additional precision does not enable management to make better decisions, additional expense for accounting cannot be justified. For this reason, some companies include minor items of variable or semi-variable cost in the period cost classification to simplify handling and reporting.

Practice seems to show that precision in the separation of direct and period costs is less important for inventory costing than it is for profit planning and cost control. Borderline costs which cause most of the difficulties in classification are often relatively small in total and can be put into either the direct or period category without material effect on inventory or income margin figures.

Several companies define direct cost for inventory costing as prime cost (i.e., direct material and direct labor cost). These companies have followed the practice of costing inventory at prime cost for many years and the reasons why prime cost was originally adopted are not known to present personnel. However, the desire to state inventory conservatively and the fact that practical methods for analyzing indirect costs into variable and period components were not yet developed probably explain the initial use of prime cost. For profit planning and cost control a more precise measurement of direct cost is needed and the same companies now include variable overhead expenses in direct cost used for purposes other than inventory costing.

Techniques for Separating Direct and Period Costs

Classification of costs into direct or period categories is usually a step in preparing the budget for a coming period. Where the variation of costs with volume has not previously been studied, a substantial amount of analysis is necessary. A number of companies participating in this study adopted direct costing at the same time they modernized their cost systems. On the other hand, where a well developed cost system employing operating cost budgets and standard costs exists, most of the basic information is available.

An earlier N.A.A. research study described three techniques for separating direct and period costs.[6] All three of these techniques are commonly used together. Practice reported by companies participating in this study is summarized below.

1. *Assignment of costs to direct or period categories by inspection of the chart of accounts.* Separation of costs into the two classes usually begins with this procedure. Where a sufficiently detailed chart of cost accounts is available, most of the accounts can be classified by this method. For example, one company described its experience as follows:

> "Because manufacturing expense was considerably detailed in the accounts prior to the adoption of direct costing, it was a reasonably simple matter to make the segregation of variable and constant costs based on judgment and an analysis of the various manufacturing cost collection areas or cost centers."

Knowledge of the operations in which each cost originates is drawn upon to guide classification by this procedure. An account which is direct in one department may be a period cost in another department. Thus, one company found that electric power cost was constant with time in all departments except the foundry where the use of power by an electric furnace varied with production. As expressed by one company representative, "Any expense may be direct or period depending upon the purpose for which it was incurred." For this reason, accounts by nature of expense are assigned to departments and then classified as direct or period according to the function performed by each department. This process is illustrated by the following example:

Expense by Type	Code No.	Functional Classification	Direct Cost	Period Cost
Salaries	01	Production Control Dept.		x
		Cost Dept.		x
Wages...direct labor	04	Small Machines Dept.	x	
		Other Production Depts.	x	
Wages...indirect labor	05	Small Machines Dept.	x	
		Cost Department		x
Social Security Taxes	15	Small Machines Dept.	x	
		Other Production Depts.	x	

---

[6] See *The Analysis of Cost-Volume-Profit Relationships*, combined Research Series Nos. 16, 17, 18, pp. 10-19.

Expense by Type	Code No.	Functional Classification	Direct Cost	Period Cost
		Production Control Dept.		x
		Cost Dept.		x
Repair & Maintenance		Cost Dept.		x
Labor	60	Production Control Dept.		x
		Small Machines Dept.	x	
		Other Production Depts.	x	
		Occupancy Dept.		x

However, some costs require analysis by methods described below. If the existing chart of accounts does not permit classification of costs in sufficient detail by products and responsibilities for control, more analysis will be needed and the chart of accounts must be revised to provide data for reports useful in profit planning and cost control.

2. *Statistical analysis of costs, using techniques such as scatter charts and mathematical methods for determining variable cost rates and amounts of fixed costs.* While these methods have been often described in accounting literature, they are seldom used by companies participating in the study. Reasons usually given were that these procedures are techniques for analyzing historical costs and do not necessarily reflect either current standard allowances per unit or per period. However, where it is desired to review past experience as a basis for setting standard costs, these techniques may be helpful. For example, one company first prepared scatter charts for manufacturing overhead expenses and then reviewed each expense to decide whether, in the future, it should be controlled with volume or with time.

3. *Industrial engineering studies to predict how costs are expected to vary with volume.* This approach entails systematic study to determine quantity of supplies, number and type of employees, and services which should be consumed at different volumes of production. The field study showed that industrial engineers often make or participate in such studies. For example, one company reported that plant industrial engineers and plant controllers working together analyzed expense accounts and made the decisions as to classification of costs into direct or period categories.

Once established, the classification of costs as direct or period is usually reviewed in the course of preparing periodic budgets. Changes in operations or in organization may affect the nature

20

of some costs and require shifting individual items from one category to the other.

Summary and Conclusion

The conclusion to be drawn from company experience is that classification of costs into direct and period categories requires judgment exercised in the light of knowledge of the principal purposes for which the resulting data will be used by management. Costs which are direct for one type of decision may be period costs for another decision, or vice versa. Where direct costing is in use, the cost classification incorporated into the accounts is usually designed for short run profit planning or current cost control. Special analyses are made when decisions at issue call for definitions of direct and period cost which differ from those used in accounting for costs where direct costing is in use.

In classifying individual cost items, consideration must be given to the nature of the related operation and to management's policy with respect to control or non-control of each cost with volume.

chapter 3

APPLICATIONS OF DIRECT COSTING IN PROFIT PLANNING

A majority of the companies participating in this study adopted direct costing primarily for its usefulness in profit planning. This chapter presents reasons why these companies have found direct costing helpful in profit planning and describes applications to some representative types of profit planning decisions.

What is Profit Planning?

Profit planning may be defined as the planning of future operations to attain a stated profit goal. The term is generally used to include both the planning and coordination of all operations toward a periodic profit objective and the evaluation and planning of individual projects in terms of their contribution to the overall objective. Periodic profit planning is illustrated by the process of preparing an annual profit budget while project profit planning deals with individual sales promotions, bids for customer orders, adding or dropping products, sales territories, customers, etc. While the term is often used broadly to include both long range planning for periods of time measured in years and short range planning for periods of a year or less, this study indicates that direct costing is much more useful in planning for short periods and in making current operating decisions than it is for long range planning.

In order to make plans which are realizable, it is necessary to measure the relationships between profit and the major factors affecting profit (sales volume, selling prices, sales mix, production and selling costs) because all of these factors are variables. Unless these relationships are known, there can be no assurance that plans and subsequent actions to control activities according to plan will lead to the anticipated profit. The Association's earlier research report on direct costing summarized the importance of the volume factor in profit planning with the following statement[7]:

> "Most managerial decisions are affected, in part at least, by the changes in costs and sales income which accompany changes in volume. For example, volume needs to be considered in decisions such as pricing products, budgeting advertising expenditures, adding or dropping products, and in making capital expenditures for new machinery. Volume is accordingly one of the key factors which must be considered in profit planning. Moreover, decisions of the type here under consideration are made frequently and the need for analysis of cost-volume-profit relationships is recurring."

One of the accountant's principal tasks in profit planning is to determine the profit consequences of a change in volume which will result from a proposed change in operations.

Key Figures in Cost-Volume-Profit Relationships

The companies using direct costing report that it facilitates the analysis of cost-volume-profit relationships because the following key figures in a company's profit structure are readily available:

1. Revenues anticipated or received from any given segment of total sales (e.g., a product, sales territory, sales order, etc.) with which a decision is concerned.

2. Direct costs incurred to secure the foregoing revenues. Since unit direct cost is constant, the amount of direct cost can easily be projected for any planned volume.

3. Marginal income from the segment under review. Since marginal income measures the rate of change in net income that accompanies change in volume of sales, the increment in net income from any planned increment in volume can be projected.

4. The amount of period cost associated with any specified period of time. These costs can be projected for the capacity which management plans to maintain for the period under consideration.

5. Net income from operations (i.e., marginal income less period costs) for any specified period of time. This net profit figure reflects planned or actual sales and costs unobscured by changes in the amount of period cost carried in inventory.

Given the key figures listed above, a wide variety of questions which arise in profit planning can be answered. Typical of such questions are the following:

1. How many units must be sold to break even, to earn a specified

---

[7] *Direct Costing*, Research Series No. 23, p. 23.

```
                    JCF Glass Company
               Standard Direct Cost Per Gross*

Date: 1/1/53        No. 240       Glass Color: Amber        Machine Type: I.S. 5
Customer            R.H.Booze Co., Philadelphia, Pa.
Description         4/5 Qt. Fancy Liquor Rd.                Register No. 7963
Carton No. & Style  4607— 1 Doz. 200# Test "A" Style        Speed-Pcs./Min.  40
Bottle Wt. in Oz. 20  Inv. Code 80  Wt. packed gross in lbs. 204   % Pack 90
                                                           Packed Gross/Hr.  15
```

	Rate Unit	Quan-tity	Material Rate	Material Amt.	Labor Rate	Labor Amt.	Expense Rate	Expense Amt.	Total Direct Cost
Glass cost	Cwt.	180 lb.	.70	1.26			.06	.11	
Feed & form-Oper. 10	Hr.	15 gr.			1.75	.12	2.00	.13	
Select and pack-Oper. 11	Hr.	15 gr.			3.60	.24	.80	.05	
Carton hdlg. - Oper. 12	M	12	201.00	2.41	16.00	.19	9.00	.10	
Warehousing-Oper. 13	Cwt.	180 lb.			.07	.13	.02	.04	
Royalty								.02	
Inventory value	Grq			3.67		.68		.45	$ 4.80
Shipping-Oper. 14	Cwt.	204#			.09	.18	.01	.02	
Total direct cost				3.67		.86		.47	5.00

```
Gross sales price                                                    $ 9.50
Freight & discount-terms F.O.B. customers plant 1%-- 10—net 30          .60
Net sales income                                                     $ 8.90
Marginal contribution per gross                                      $ 3.90
Marginal contribution—%                                                43.8
Marginal contribution per hr.       ($3.90 x 15 gross per hr.)        $58.50
```

*From "Direct costing in a Glass Container Plant," Ray E. Longenecker, N.A.(C)A. Bulletin,
June 1953, p. 1284.

Exhibit 1

amount of profit, or a desired rate of return on investment?

2. How much will a given segment of total sales contribute to over-all profit?

3. What will the over-all net profit from operations be if a given volume of sales is realized?

The preceding questions turn upon volume with other factors assumed to remain constant. More often, changes in selling prices, sales mix, and costs occur together with volume changes to produce more complex questions such as those listed below:

4. Will profits be increased by a price increase which reduces sales volume or by a price decrease to expand volume?

5. Will added volume obtained by additional advertising and sales promotion be profitable?

6. Which products or customers should be emphasized in attempts to improve sales mix?

7. What effect will changes in the company's cost structure (e.g., increased automation which decreases direct cost and increases period costs and investment) have on profits under conditions of varying volume?

Statement of Earnings
Product Division A - Month of February, 1959
(000 Omitted)

	Actual	%	Profit Plan	%	Variance
Gross sales	$2 700		$2 100		$+600
Returns & allowances	200		100		-100
Net sales	$2 500	100.0	$2 000	100.0	$+500
Variable cost of sales:					
Inventory	$1 450		$1 075		$-375
Other var. costs	50		25		- 25
Variable margin	$1 000	40.0	$ 900	45.0	$+100
Period costs:					
Manufacturing	$ 300		$ 275		$- 25
Selling	125		115		- 10
Administrative	75		80		+ 5
Engineering	150		120		- 30
Total period costs	$ 650		$ 590		$- 60
Controllable earnings	$ 350	14.0	$ 310	15.5	$+ 40
Inventory adjustment					
Period cost complement	90*		80*		- 10
Earnings before taxes	$ 260	10.4	$ 230	11.5	$+ 30

* This amount represents the net change in the amount of capacity or period
  cost allocated to inventory for the current month.

Exhibit 2

Short-Run vs. Long-Run Planning

Short-run profit planning is concerned with comparatively small segments of total volume which are within the limits of established capacity or with periods of time which are too short to permit major changes in capacity to be made. Under such conditions it is realistic to assume that total period cost will remain constant.

The direct cost and marginal income figures need to be available with a minimum of additional analysis in order that decisions can be made before opportunities are lost. Where direct costing is in use, product cost records and recent income statements serve as the basic source of data. Exhibit 1 illustrates a product cost card of the type commonly used where process costing is employed and Exhibit 15 shows a job order cost sheet. In some companies departmental step budgets are also prepared to cover planned changes in period costs which will be occasioned by events such as a change in the number of shifts worked or length of the work week. After a budget plan has been put into operation, actual costs and income margins recorded in the ac-

25

counts can be compared directly with the corresponding planned figures. Hence it can be said that direct costing integrates accounting for historical profits with planning for future profits. A product division earnings statement illustrating this comparison of actual results with planned results is shown in Exhibit 2.

On the other hand, long-run profit planning involves volume changes which are relatively large and which persist for extended periods of time. Such changes may be expected to alter the present period costs. For example, a decision to refuse a small order for Product A will probably have no effect on total period costs, but a decision to abandon the product will eliminate period costs specifically related to the product through actions such as disposal of machinery used only for the product and the consequent termination of depreciation, property taxes, and similar charges. On the other hand, a large increase in sales of Product A will probably require expansion of capacity with an increase in total period cost. Unit direct cost may also be changed if, for example, the increased output is accompanied by greater mechanization of operations.

While costs recorded in the accounts must be adjusted to reflect any anticipated changes, companies using direct costing reported that separation of direct and period components facilitates the necessary adjustment and projection of data taken from the accounts. They also stated that usefulness of cost reports for decision making is improved by showing separately those period costs which are specific to the product (or other segment) and those period costs which are shared in common with other products. An example of such a statement is shown in Exhibit 3.

No clear line of demarcation exists between short and long run situations, for they are points of view that shade from one into another. Consequently, each plan or project should be reviewed to determine whether or not actions proposed will change currently established period cost.

Comparative Advantages of Direct Costing For Profit Planning

Before adopting direct costing, most of the companies participating in this study had kept their accounts on an absorption costing basis without separation of direct and period costs. These companies found their absorption costing systems to have distinct shortcomings for providing data needed in making de-

Product Line Income Statement

	Total Amount	Total Pct.	Product Lines No. 1 Amount	No. 1 Pct.	No. 2 Amount	No. 2 Pct.	No. 3 Amount	No. 3 Pct.
Net sales	$600,000	100.0	$300,000	100.0	$200,000	100.0	$100,000	100.0
Direct costs								
Manufacturing								
Direct materials.........	$150,000	25.0	$ 75,000	25.0	$ 55,000	27.5	20,000	20.0
Direct labor	90,000	15.0	30,000	10.0	30,000	15.0	30,000	30.0
Direct overhead	60,000	10.0	30,000	10.0	20,000	10.0	10,000	10.0
Selling								
Freight out.........	12,000	2.0	9,000	3.0	3,000	1.5	----	----
Salesmen's commissions.........	24,000	4.0	12,000	4.0	8,000	4.0	4,000	4.0
Total direct costs........	$336,000	56.0	$156,000	52.0	$116,000	58.0	64,000	64.0
Marginal income.........	$264,000	44.0	$144,000	48.0	$ 84,000	42.0	$ 36,000	36.0
Period costs specific to product lines								
Depreciation.........	$ 40,000		$ 20,000		$ 10,000		$ 10,000	
Property taxes & insurance.......	20,000		10,000		2,000		8,000	
Advertising.........	24,000		20,000		---		4,000	
Total.........	$ 84,000		$ 50,000		$ 12,000		$ 22,000	
Margin after specific period costs	$180,000	30.0	$ 94,000	31.3	$ 72,000	36.0	14,000	14.0
Allocated general period costs								
Manufacturing	$ 40,000		$ 20,000		$ 13,320		$ 6,680	
Selling.........	30,000		15,000		10,000		5,000	
Administrative	30,000		15,000		10,000		5,000	
Research & development.........	20,000		10,000		6,666		3,334	
Total.........	$120,000		$ 60,000		$ 39,986		20,014	
Profit (loss) before taxes.........	$ 60,000	10.0	$ 34,000	10.3	$ 32,014	16.5	($ 6,014)	(6.0)

Exhibit 3

27

cisions where volume was a variable factor. The shortcomings described had their origin in the fact that, under absorption costing systems used by these companies, product costs were based upon a single volume and rates at which costs and profits changed with volume could be ascertained only by analysis.

It was further stated that the analysis required to determine profit consequences of volume increments was usually difficult and consumed the time of skilled accountants.[8] For example, one company representative stated that, before direct costing was adopted, it was necessary to recompute burden absorption through twenty cost centers to determine how much a given order would add to the company's profit. In addition, comparison of forecasted profits with actual profit subsequently reported was difficult because, under absorption costing, profits were influenced by changes in the inventory of manufactured goods as well as by changes in sales volume. As a consequence, analyses were made only for major decisions. Decisions of smaller scope and decisions which had to be made quickly were made without the financial data needed to guide them. Among the many other examples provided by companies participating in the field study, the following are typical:

1. A company manufactured products having distinctly seasonal demand. Opportunities were available to obtain low-priced, off-season orders which would not compete with the more profitable peak season business. However, acting on the basis of

---

[8] The reasons why this analysis was considered difficult can be seen by reviewing the problems which arise in determining the change in profit expected to result from a change in sales volume of one product produced by a multi-product company:

1. If predetermined overhead rates are not used, a change in volume for one product will change the amount of period cost absorbed and profit shown by all other products going through the same cost centers. A decrease in volume for one product may increase the amount of period cost charged to other products to such an extent that products which had been profitable before may subsequently appear to be sold at a loss. Such figures might lead management to abandon products which were absorbing a portion of the period costs and thereby to decrease the company's overall profit. Only by comparing the aggregate profit on all products combined, both before and after the volume change, can the correct change in profit be determined.

2. If overhead rates are based on standard or normal volume, changes in volume do not affect standard cost of individual products. However, deviations from standard volume give rise to overhead absorption variances which affect overall profit. Since these variances relate to all production going through a cost center during the period, it is virtually impossible to determine how much of the variance applies to any one order or product except by allocations which are not reliable enough to form the basis for decision making.

28

product costs in its possession, management rejected orders which did not show a profit over cost including overhead applied at rates based on normal volume. Introduction of direct costing disclosed the fact that many of these orders would make a positive contribution to annual period costs and consequently increase the company's annual profits. These gains were increased by improved labor efficiency which followed more stable employment. While management had long wished to avoid the seasonal curtailment of production, it had lacked the type of information which enabled it to determine within close limits which off-season orders would add to the company's annual profit.

2. Another company manufacturing several lines of consumer products frequently used sales promotions and price reduction deals of limited scope designed to stimulate immediate customer response. Proposals for such promotions were usually accepted or rejected principally on the basis of the volume of sales expected to result. To estimate profit was considered impractical because proposals were often developed and decisions made in the course of a single conference. After the introduction of direct costing, the additional volume required to offset proposed added sales expense or reduced sales revenue could easily be calculated while the proposal was being discussed. Some plans which would probably have been accepted previously were now promptly discarded when it was seen that the added costs could not be recovered even though the most optimistic forecasts of added volume were realized.

Management may fail to realize that costing rates prepared by absorption costing methods hold only for the specific volume used in computing the costs. Such misinterpretation can lead to erroneous decisions. The following examples from the field study illustrate this statement:

In one company it was discovered that operations were being performed by hand when automatic machines were available and that orders were scheduled on old machines in preference to newer and more efficient machines. Investigation showed that supervisors used hand labor to avoid being charged with the high hourly rates carried by automatic machines. They also believed that the old machines were more economical because they carried lower overhead rates owing to the fact that they were fully depreciated in the accounts. Management here did not realize that the high machine hour rates consisted largely of period costs which were not reduced by non-use of the equipment and that the decisions made increased the company's out-of-pocket costs unnecessarily.

Another company decided to increase its inventory of manufactured goods during a period of low sales volume. The principal factor leading to this decision was management's desire to avoid the drop in profits which would result if production were curtailed. Subsequently management realized that the same goods could have been produced later with a substantial saving in carrying charges on capital tied up in direct costs of the inventory. At the same time it was seen that period costs absorbed by production had not been saved by merely postponing the charge against revenues. Opinion was expressed to the effect that the introduction of direct costing had given management a clearer understanding of the financial consequences of such decisions.

It is, of course, possible to develop direct and period costs for profit planning as supplementary statistics apart from the accounts where the latter are kept on an absorption costing basis. Company representatives interviewed commonly expressed the opinion that a disadvantage of the statistical approach is that it often appears to be in conflict with the accounts. For example, orders which make a contribution to period costs and profits may appear unprofitable when the selling price is compared with cost computed by usual absorption costing methods. The relative desirability of individual products in a group may also be quite different when ranked by marginal income and by net profit. These apparent paradoxes are, of course, not real because both approaches yield the same answer if the absorption costing calculations are carried out to reflect the effect of changed volume on overall net profit for the period and the direct cost profit is adjusted for changes in fixed cost content of the inventory. Nevertheless, it was stated that management is sometimes confused and uncertain about what action it should take. Experience of all companies participating in this study shows that management finds it easier to understand cost and income margin data presented in direct costing form. This fact probably explains why, in several interviews, it was stated that pressure to intrcduce direct costing came from the administrative, manufacturing, and sales sections of the companies rather than from the financial sections. At the same time, the actions which management is led to take on the basis of data in direct costing form are the same as those indicated by the same data in absorption costing form provided the latter is correctly understood.

Examples of Direct Costing in Profit Planning

In describing applications of profit planning it is helpful to distinguish changes in sales volume, selling prices, sales mix, and costs even though, in practice, changes in several of these factors usually occur in combination. The following examples are chosen to illustrate applications of direct costing in evaluating the effects which each of the foregoing factors has on profit.[9] However, a discussion of direct costing in connection with pricing appears in Chapter 4.

Evaluating Profit Consequences of Volume Changes

Virtually all companies have, at some time, capacity which is not fully utilized. Under such conditions, overall profit can be increased by using this otherwise idle capacity to make and sell goods which return a positive marginal income. The increment in marginal income then measures the addition of net operating profit made by the increment in volume of sales.

Additional volume may be sought in many ways—for example, by adding new products that can be made with equipment now partially utilized, by extending sales of present products into new markets, by inducing present customers to buy more, etc. However, such additional volume is usually obtained at higher costs or lower selling prices. Therefore, management is faced with the need to decide whether or not an anticipated increase in sales revenue will produce an acceptable addition to profits. As a basis for such decisions, analyses of relevant revenue and costs are made in the following form by one company:

Introduction of a new product was proposed to make use of manufacturing capacity which was idle. The following estimate of sales and costs was prepared for the product:

Standard direct material, per unit	$	1.00
Standard direct labor, per unit		.10
Standard variable manufacturing expense		.90
Total direct cost	$	2.00
Competitive selling price	$	3.40
Marginal income, per unit	$	1.40
Expected sales, per month		10,000 units
Profit contribution, per month	$ 14,000	

In preparing the above estimates, it was ascertained that sufficient plant capacity was available and that fixed expenses would not increase. Direct cost of the product was developed from specifications of the product and from recorded direct costs of cost centers in which the new product would be made.

On the basis of this analysis, it was stated that "No question—we would want this business. Under whole costs, we would not know the profit contribution of this product except by recalculating our costs and breaking out the fixed expense. Frequently, there

---

[9] For additional discussion of this topic, see *The Analysis of Cost-Volume-Profit Relationships*, combined Research Series Nos. 16, 17, 18, Chapter 2.

31

is not time to do this before we quote. We would decide under whole costs that we do not want this business, not knowing it would contribute $14,000."

Another approach to profit improvement is through increased sales effort applied to present products. Regarding this, one company representative commented that:

"The value of increased and perhaps more costly selling efforts directed at any one product can be more easily tested before the money is spent because marginal income from the anticipated sales increase is known."

Projecting Profit Results from Change in Sales Mix

One of the main advantages advanced for direct costing is that it helps management to determine which products are the most profitable to sell. These are the products that return the largest marginal income per unit. The following comment was made by a company representative in one of the field interviews:

"This problem is greatly simplified by direct costing because profitability of products, sales territories, customers, and other segments of the business can be measured without regard to a specific volume of business. Within a reasonable range of activity, variable cost and marginal income per unit remain constant. With use of the marginal income ratio, profitability of a large number of closely associated products can be readily determined. Sales efforts can then be directed to choose products providing the greatest contribution toward constant costs and profit."

When the volume of goods that can be sold exceeds the production capacity of available machines, the highest net profit results from using machine capacity to produce those products which return the largest marginal income per machine hour. As may be seen from Exhibit 4, the products yielding the highest marginal income per sales dollar are not necessarily the most profitable per machine hour. This is especially true where products made on the same machines have to be processed at different rates of speed. While plant and equipment are most commonly the factors which limit short run production, labor or materials may, on occasion, be the limiting factors. If the available labor supply is inadequate to permit manufacture of all the goods that can be sold, the most profitable course of action is to use the available manpower to make the products which return the largest marginal income per hour of labor. Likewise if materials are in short supply, management may wish to produce those products which yield the highest marginal income per unit of

32

Analysis of Sales and Marginal Income by Products

MONTH: January, 1960

	Sales		Direct	Marginal Income				
					Cents	Per machine hour		
		Pct. of	standard		per sales	Dollar		Pct. of target
Products	Amount	total	cost	Total	dollar	amount	Rank	($140 per Hr.)
A	$ 50,400	5.9%	$ 26,208	$ 24,192	48.0	$ 154.30	2	110.2%
B	136,800	16.5	75,514	61,286	44.8	135.75	4	96.9
C	82,380	9.7	47,368	35,012	42.5	142.50	3	101.7
D	48,700	5.7	29,512	19,188	39.4	122.65	6	87.6
E	243,200	28.6	156,678	86,522	35.7	129.25	5	92.3
F	75,180	8.3	51,047	24,133	32.1	110.95	7	79.2
G	125,250	14.7	93,687	31,563	25.2	210.80	1	150.6
H	90,310	10.6	73,693	16,617	18.4	93.20	8	66.5
	$852,220	100.0%	$553,707	$298,513	35.0			

Exhibit 4

Income Statement by Sales Districts

	Total Company	Sales Districts A	B	C	D
Sales	$2,500,000	$900,000	$700,000	$500,000	$400,000
Direct variable costs:					
Product	$1,250,000	450,000	350,000	250,000	200,000
Selling	395,000	90,000	105,000	100,000	100,000
	$1,645,000	$540,000	$455,000	$350,000	$300,000
Variable profit	$ 855,000	$360,000	$245,000	$150,000	$100,000
District period costs	645,000	180,000	175,000	150,000	140,000
Profit or (Loss) by districts	210,000	$180,000	$ 70,000	-0-	$(40,000)
General company period costs	140,000				
Profit before taxes	$ 70,000				

Exhibit 5

material.[10] For this purpose, Frederick J. Muth has written that direct costing is helpful for:[11]

"The sharper focus that is obtained on relative profitability of product lines, types of customers, and territories pinpoints the areas where management should concentrate its efforts and where to weed out the unprofitable items. This is especially important when facilities are being used at near-capacity levels."

The general rule is to express marginal income in terms of the factor that limits the volume of business that can be done. In one company this is termed the "effective marginal income." As noted above, this factor may be sales, plant capacity, labor, or materials according to the circumstances.

Direct costing is helpful in developing data to show which sales territories, customers, or other segments are contributing the most marginal income. Exhibit 5 shows a statement prepared by one company to evaluate sales districts. In this statement, sales are first tabulated by district and direct variable costs (both product and selling) are deducted to give marginal income earned by each district. This figure is, of course, variable with sales and measures the increment in profit which will result from any increase in sales of the individual district. The next step is to deduct the period costs which are specific to individual districts (warehouse and office rentals, salesmen's salaries, etc.) from marginal income to obtain "Profit or Loss by Districts." This figure is the contribution made by the districts to general company period costs and profits. The same figure also measures the financial consequences of eliminating a district. For example, in Exhibit 5, elimination of District D would increase over-all company profit by $40,000 a year. General period costs common to all districts are not allocated to districts by the company that supplied Exhibit 5 because it is believed that the results would not serve any useful purpose.

The field study disclosed a few companies which are developing plans to compensate salesmen on the basis of the marginal income which each man produces. In these companies management believes that this will give the sales force a financial incentive to push those products which add the most to company profits. Studies of salesmen's performance made by one company showed that the salesmen who ranked first in volume of

---

[10] For more complete discussion see George L. Faulkner, "Profit Analysis For The Magnet Wire Industry", N.A.(C.)A. Bulletin, September, 1952.

[11] "An Evaluation of Direct Costing", The Controller, February, 1957, p. 64.

sales did not always stand equally high when measured on the basis of their contribution to profits. If, by such a change in the compensation plan, salesmen can be motivated to sell a larger proportion of items yielding high marginal income, the company's profits should improve. At the same time, salesmen will be more equitably rewarded because their earnings will reflect their contribution to the company's profits rather than volume alone. In order to lay a foundation for such a compensation plan, one company regularly supplies each salesman with statistics showing marginal income on his sales and the amount he would have earned under the proposed plan. These figures are discussed at sales meetings to develop understanding and acceptance of the plan before it is put into effect.

The foregoing examples reflect a short-range point of view in that it has been assumed that changes in volume do not exceed the range within which period costs remain stable. In making profit planning decisions, long range aspects of the problem under consideration should not be ignored. The most profitable course in the long run may be to forego certain short run profit opportunities. For example, a new product or sales district which is currently unprofitable will not be dropped if it is expected to develop into a profitable one in the future. In general, questions such as those listed below should be answered before making decisions:

1. Will attempts to increase volume by means such as limited use of price reductions or deals spoil the market for more profitable items or provoke retaliation by competitors?
2. Will proposed changes (e.g., elimination of a low margin product) unfavorably affect the sales of other items?
3. Can control over sales mix be maintained to limit production and sales of less profitable items to the volume needed to utilize capacity for which a more profitable use is lacking?
4. Will it be necessary to add a shift, to expand the plant, or to hire more salaried employees and thereby increase period costs, either now or in the future?
5. Have all alternatives been reviewed to discover other opportunities which might be more profitable?

Decision Making in the Manufacturing Area

Management frequently has occasion to make decisions with respect to operating alternatives in the factory. Many of these decisions are quite limited in scope and involve only minor changes in facilities and organization which are the sources of period costs. Those period costs which will be unchanged in total regardless of which alternative is chosen are not relevant to the decision. For this reason, direct costing was often reported to be helpful because less analysis is needed to develop costs in a form which can serve as basic data for decisions to make or buy, to own or lease equipment, how far to go in automating a process, and many others. The same data are also useful in studies intended to determine the effect on earnings of proposed changes in product design, manufacturing methods, and other changes affecting product cost.

Make or Buy Decisions

If a company has unused capacity, the additional cost of making component parts or similar items consists of material, variable labor, and direct expense such as power, supplies, fringe benefits, etc. Even a large portion of direct labor cost may be properly excluded in cases where the work can be assigned to skilled employees (e.g. machinists or toolmakers) during times when they would otherwise be idle. Such employees are often not released during temporary periods of low activity because they are difficult to replace when needed. The cost to be compared with prices quoted by outside vendors should be the amount of cost to make which will not be incurred if the item is purchased. This cost may vary from time to time, for during periods of low volume capacity may be available for added production at low out-of-pocket cost while in periods of high volume it may be necessary to work overtime or acquire more equipment before additional work can be undertaken.

Several company representatives commented that, even if the company ordinarily intends to purchase, a knowledge of the direct cost of making items in the company's own plant is useful in judging prices quoted by suppliers. Direct cost of manufacturing had also been used to show union representatives why increased productivity was needed to maintain an economical operation in comparison with prices quoted by potential suppliers.

Other Uses in Manufacturing Area

Availability of information with regard to behavior of manufacturing costs under conditions of varying volume has, it was stated, led to better operating decisions in companies participating in the study. The following example is given for illustration:

> One company had recently acquired highly automated equipment to produce in a single operation a product which had previously required a series of hand operations. However, the older manu-

facturing method was continued in use because the new equipment
had not been designed to supply all of the production needed
during peak seasonal operations. Comparative operating costs of
the two types of equipment are illustrated by the hypothetical
figure below:

	New Equipment	*Old Equipment*
Direct cost —per unit		
Material	$ 5.00	$ 5.00
Labor	2.00	10.00
Variable expense	.50	2.00
Total direct cost	$ 7.50	$ 17.00
Period cost—per month	$ 12,500	$ 3,000

With the above cost data in view, factory management sees that
the old equipment should be operated only when the new equipment is fully occupied because additional production from the
new machine costs only $7.50 per unit in comparison with $17.00
per unit from the old equipment. However, for the purpose of
costing finished goods inventory in external financial reports,
this product is assigned a unit cost of $20.00 (based on a standard
volume of 1,000 units per month) regardless of which equipment
is used to produce it.

Although none of the companies participating in this study
had made extensive use of operations research, other companies
have found that direct costing facilitates the use of cost records
as a source of data for operations research studies to determine
optimum production schedules, inventory policy, and similar
questions. The reason for this is that such studies involve comparing alternatives in terms of costs which are variable with
independent factors such as volume.

Developing a Coordinated Profit Plan

The preceding pages of this chapter have described uses of
direct costing in making decisions with respect to specific questions or projects. Such individual decisions need to be integrated
into a periodic profit plan coordinating all activities. Exhibit 6
shows an illustration prepared by one company to present to its
management the principal steps in profit planning. This illustration assumes that both standard costs and direct costing are in
use. Hence, in developing planned costs, production is costed
at standard direct cost and period costs for both manufacturing
and non-manufacturing functions are taken from capacity cost
budgets. The latter give effect to the anticipated level of operations, facilities available, and program with respect to maintenance of an organization.

Development of Typical Profit Plan
(To Operating Earnings Level Only)

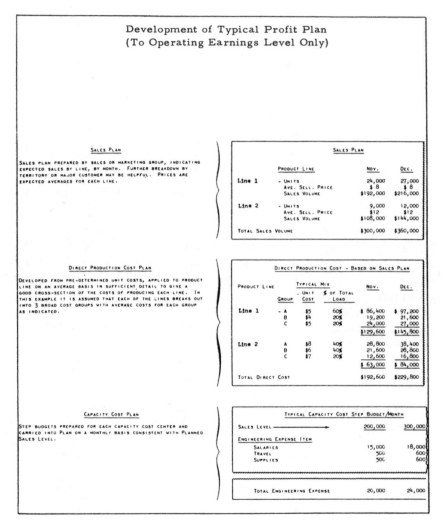

SALES PLAN

Sales plan prepared by sales or marketing group, indicating expected sales by line, by month. Further breakdown by territory or major customer may be helpful. Prices are expected averages for each line.

SALES PLAN

PRODUCT LINE		NOV.	DEC.
Line 1	- UNITS	24,000	27,000
	AVE. SELL. PRICE	$ 8	$ 8
	SALES VOLUME	$192,000	$216,000
Line 2	- UNITS	9,000	12,000
	AVE. SELL. PRICE	$12	$12
	SALES VOLUME	$108,000	$144,000
TOTAL SALES VOLUME		$300,000	$360,000

DIRECT PRODUCTION COST PLAN

Developed from pre-determined unit costs, applied to product line on an average basis in sufficient detail to give a good cross-section of the costs of producing each line. In this example it is assumed that each of the lines breaks out into 3 broad cost groups with average costs for each group as indicated.

DIRECT PRODUCTION COST - BASED ON SALES PLAN

PRODUCT LINE		TYPICAL MIX		NOV.	DEC.
	GROUP	UNIT COST	% OF TOTAL LOAD		
Line 1	- A	$5	60%	$ 86,400	$ 97,200
	B	$4	20%	19,200	21,600
	C	$5	20%	24,000	27,000
				$129,600	$145,800
Line 2	A	$8	40%	28,800	38,400
	B	$6	40%	21,600	28,800
	C	$7	20%	12,600	16,800
				$ 63,000	$ 84,000
TOTAL DIRECT COST				$192,600	$229,800

CAPACITY COST PLAN

Step budgets prepared for each capacity cost center and carried into Plan on a monthly basis consistent with planned sales level.

TYPICAL CAPACITY COST STEP BUDGET/MONTH

SALES LEVEL ⟶	200,000	300,000
ENGINEERING EXPENSE ITEM		
SALARIES	15,000	18,000
TRAVEL	500	600
SUPPLIES	500	600
TOTAL ENGINEERING EXPENSE	20,000	24,000

Exhibit 6

Development of Typical Profit Plan
(To Operating Earnings Level Only)

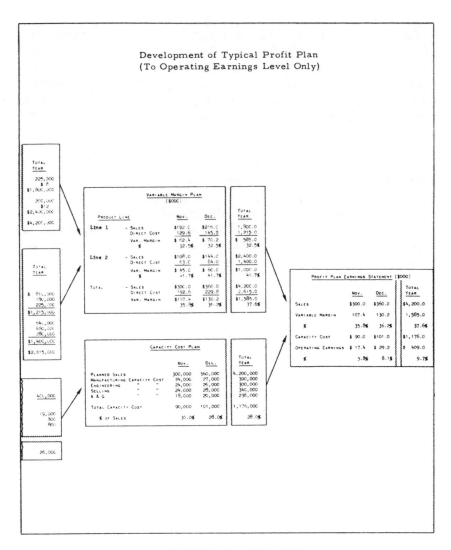

Exhibit 6—(Cont'd)

Summary and Conclusion

The usefulness which direct costing was expected to have for short-run profit planning was the principal reason why most of the fifty companies participating in this study adopted direct costing. All reported that the advantages anticipated have or will be realized.

Since volume is a variable factor in planning, knowledge of cost-volume-profit relationships facilitates planning. By knowing the rate at which profit varies with volume (i.e., the marginal income ratio), management can determine the expected addition to profit from a proposed increment in volume when the capacity provided by period costs is not fully utilized. The same data also provide a guide to selecting the most profitable products, customers, or other segments when the available volume of business exceeds capacity of existing facilities.

Moreover, participants in the study generally agreed that it is advantageous in profit planning to have direct and period costs accumulated separately in the accounts rather than to develop this cost classification as statistics supplementing accounts kept on an absorption basis. The major reason stems from the fact that when period manufacturing costs are absorbed by production, unit gross and net profit margins are valid only for the specific volume on which period costs are unitized. On the other hand, unit marginal income figures hold for any volume within the range for which period costs remain constant. Under direct costing, management can use actual and budgeted product cost and income statements without need for analysis to bring out cost-profit-volume relationships or for reconciliations between data used for decision making and results shown in the accounts.

chapter 4

APPLICATIONS OF DIRECT COSTING TO GUIDE PRICING DECISIONS

An earlier N.A.A. research study found that while cost is usually looked upon as the starting point in pricing, selling prices do not have an inflexible relationship to cost.[12] In pricing, elasticity of customer demand, competition, and the nature of the product are factors that enter into the pricing decision along with costs of manufacturing and marketing.

Moreover, product cost for pricing is not a single figure, but instead is a series of figures showing the effects of alternative combinations of price, volume, and other variable factors. Management's objective usually is to find the combination of price and volume which yields the best rate of return on investment. The accountant's responsibility is to supply cost and income margin data relevant to the decisions at issue and to counsel management in the meaning and use of such data.

Relationship Between Direct Costs and Selling Prices

Ordinarily a company does not long continue selling a product at a price below direct cost except where such sales help to sell other products which are profitable. The direct cost can, of course, be saved if the product is not produced. Hence direct cost sets a lower limit to selling price. Direct cost of a product, sales order, or other unit is usually readily determinable when direct costing is in use.

Relationship Between Period Costs and Selling Prices

In contrast with direct cost, the recovery of period costs in selling prices poses a complex and difficult problem because a substantial portion of the period costs cannot be specifically iden-

---

[12] *Product Costs for Pricing Purposes*, Research Series No. 24, Chapter 2.

41

tified with individual products or sales orders. This characteristic stems from the fact that facilities and organization which carry period costs are shared in common by different products and sales orders. For this reason period costs are often joint rather than separable.

The condition of joint cost extends to successive units in output of a single product as well as to different products produced together. The reason for this is that, unlike direct cost, the amount of period cost is not reduced by curtailing production nor is it increased by expanding production within a limited volume range. Consequently, when dropping a product or refusing an order reduces the total volume of production and sales, the same amount of period cost must be absorbed by revenues from the remaining sales. Conversely, additional sales volume within capacity of existing facilities requires no additional period cost. While accepting an order at a price below direct cost leaves the company with fewer dollars than it would have had if the goods had not been produced, any sale which makes a positive contribution to period costs leaves the company with more dollars than it would have had without the sale.

Products and orders often differ in the contribution they can make to the common pool of period costs, and these differences may change from time to time. The causes of such differences lie in customer demand. For this reason, period costs are often recovered by dividing the market into segments according to ability to contribute to the company's total period cost. These segments may be products, classes of customers, sales territories, or other segments of total sales. In pricing, some of these segments are expected to contribute more to period costs than are other segments. The ability to contribute on the part of individual segments is determined by market demand and does not necessarily correspond with the benefits received from common cost factors as measured by bases which the accountant uses to allocate common period costs. Even though selling price is uniform, markets and customers often do not contribute equally to period costs because direct costs of getting and filling orders (e.g., selling expenses, freight outward) vary with location and other characteristics of the market.

The characteristics of period costs described above make it particularly important for management to have cost and income margin data which show clearly the consequences of proposed pricing decisions. Regardless of the plan of accounting used, there seems to be need for distinction between direct and period costs wherever pricing alternatives under consideration involve differing volumes of production and sales.

Income Margins for Evaluating Selling Prices

There are two approaches to the development of unit income margins for evaluating the expected result from proposed selling prices. These are:

1. The net profit approach. Here period costs are spread uniformly over some chosen sales volume (which may be actual or standard) to arrive at an average cost per unit. When this allocated period cost is combined with the direct cost of the unit, a "full" unit cost is obtained for comparison with the proposed unit selling price. However, the indicated net profit per unit rests upon the assumption made with respect to the number of units which will be made and sold. Consequently, specific unit cost and profit figures hold only for the one volume chosen in computing these figures.[13]

2. The marginal income approach. By this method, the unit direct cost is deducted from the proposed selling price to determine the marginal income per unit. This unit marginal income figure is the change in total profit that accompanies a unit change in volume. It may be interpreted as follows:

    a. If total sales volume is less than the breakeven volume, marginal income measures the amount of period cost recovered by sale of the unit in question. If the unit is not sold, the over-all net loss will be greater by the amount of marginal income associated with the unit in question.

    b. If total sales volume currently exceeds the breakeven volume, marginal income measures the addition to over-all net profit which will result from sale of the unit in question. Since unit direct cost and marginal income are constant within the volume range for which total period cost remains stable, total income for any chosen volume can be ascertained without recomputing unit cost.

The net profit approach logically goes with absorption costing techniques in the accounts. However, in practice full unit cost is often not determined and pricing decisions are guided by unit gross margin (i.e., selling price minus manufacturing cost) rather than by unit net profit.

On the other hand, the marginal income approach to pricing follows the same reasoning as does direct costing in accounting

---

[13] For example, if cost based on standard volume is $.60 and the proposed selling price is $1.00 there is no assurance that a profit will be made by selling at this price because it is necessary to sell enough units to recover period costs before there is any profit. Only when both production and sales are exactly at standard volume will the profit of $.40 per unit be realized.

for costs. The greater accessibility of direct cost and marginal income data for pricing decisions was one of the principal reasons why a number of the companies participating in this study adopted direct costing. However, direct costing does not imply use of any particular pricing policy or method.

It is, of course, possible to arrive at the same end result (i.e., the change in overall net profit which will result from accepting an increment of business at a proposed price) by following either the absorption or direct costing routes. However, company experience reviewed in this study indicates that these routes are usually not equally convenient or practical.

Treating Volume as a Variable Factor in Pricing

The selling prices set on a company's products influence the volume of business that can be obtained and hence pricing cannot be considered apart from sales volume. Whether the pricing problem is to find the most profitable combination of volume and price for a product or to determine how much an increment at a given price will add to profit, the analyst's task is to estimate the profit that can be expected from alternative price-volume combinations.

Average actual unit cost changes with volume and consequently getting a specific sales order affects the cost of filling the order even though the effect of volume changes may be reflected in an overhead absorption variance rather than in standard production cost. To recompute period cost absorbed may be too laborious to be practical when many relatively small changes in volume are to be evaluated.

No recomputation of overhead absorption is necessary under direct costing because direct and period costs are not combined. For this reason, companies participating in this study reported that direct costing is particularly useful in circumstances where it is necessary to make frequent and prompt pricing decisions with regard to individual orders.

Company Practice in Use of Direct Costing for Pricing

Profits depend upon a proper balance of selling prices, mix, volume, and costs. For this reason, pricing decisions encompass more than the setting of figures at which products are offered to customers. In practice, prices are considered simultaneously with characteristics of products offered, terms on which they are sold, channels through which sold, and methods of selling and promotion. This can be seen in the following list of pricing problems to which direct costing has been applied by companies participating in this study:

1. Pricing individual products.
2. Finding the most profitable products.
3. Identifying products needing attention for profit improvement.
4. Improving sales mix.
5. Evaluating proposals to increase profits by increasing volume.
6. Deciding how far to go in meeting competitive prices.
7. Improving understanding of costs by management responsible for pricing.

Practice shows that the problems listed above vary in importance from company to company according to the conditions under which products are manufactured and sold. Where selling prices are established in the market and an individual company has little or no scope for independent action in pricing, product costs are not needed for setting selling prices because the only alternatives are to sell at the prevailing price or to withdraw from the market. Here costs serve principally to aid in improving the sales mix and for determining how much cost can be incurred without sacrificing profit. Similar conditions prevail where costs are largely joint and reliable product costs cannot be determined. On the other hand, where a company is a price leader in its industry or has products which are sufficiently differentiated from competing products to permit independent pricing, then product costs are usually wanted as a guide to setting selling prices.

Costs for Pricing Individual Products

Where direct costing is in use, the determination of product price for pricing requires the following figures:

1. Direct unit cost of the product.
2. Annual amount of period cost associated with the product.
3. Desired profit margin expressed in terms of return on capital or sales.

The procedure is illustrated below by a simplified example:

Data available:

Standard direct cost of product per unit	$9.00
Budgeted period cost per year	$ 40,000.00
Capital employed	$100,000.00
Desired rate of return	20%

45

Assuming 10,000 units a year can be sold, the required unit marginal income is:

$$\frac{\$40,000 + \$20,000}{10,000} = \$6.00$$

Adding marginal income to direct cost, the following selling price is indicated:

Direct cost	$ 9.00	60%
Marginal income	6.00	40%
Selling price	$15.00	100%

Similar calculations are generally made at several alternative volumes. As explained by a company representative:

"Direct costing doesn't eliminate the problem of choosing a volume on which to recover period cost. But, since we have been using direct costing, management has found it much easier to see the effect of alternative volume assumptions on cost. To decide on what volume to unitize period cost for pricing products is a decision that should be made by management rather than by the accountant."

One company uses pricing guides of the type shown in Exhibit 7. The same procedures can, of course, be used for testing present or proposed prices, after direct product costs have been determined.

Contrary to opinion sometimes expressed, the study revealed that period costs are usually assigned to products for pricing purposes by companies using direct costing. This assignment is made statistically, commonly in the course of preparing the annual budget. The amount of period costs so assigned are those anticipated for the budgeted volume and mix of sales. However, the period costs are not unitized at this stage, but are simply assigned to products as annual totals. This avoids tying product costs to a single volume and permits management to test various proposed price-volume combinations as illustrated in the example above.

In assigning the period costs to products, it seems desirable to distinguish between period costs which are traceable to specific products and period costs which are shared in common with other products. Costs of the latter type can be assigned only by allocation. The reliability of allocated costs is generally lower than it is for period costs assigned by direct charge because the decision as to what basis for allocation is "fair" or "equitable" is necessarily subjective. This separation enables management to distinguish between components of product cost which are measured with high reliability and components which are measured with low reliability.

Pricing Guide—Product Line A

Marginal Contribution Required Per Machine Hour

To Earn This Return on Capital	73% Capacity	80% Capacity	90% Capacity	100% Capacity
15%	$63.65	$60.14	$57.39	$54.92
14	62.18	58.74	56.04	53.61
13	60.70	57.34	54.68	52.29
12	59.23	55.94	53.33	50.98
11	57.75	54.54	51.97	49.67
10	56.28	53.14	50.62	48.36
9	54.80	51.74	49.27	47.04
8	53.33	50.34	47.91	45.73
7	51.85	48.94	46.56	44.42
6	50.38	47.54	45.20	43.10
5	48.90	46.14	43.85	41.79
4	47.43	44.74	42.50	40.48
3	45.95	43.34	41.14	39.16
2	44.48	41.94	39.79	37.85
1	43.00	40.54	38.43	36.54
Breakeven	41.53	39.14	37.08	35.22

Data

	73% Capacity	80% Capacity	90% Capacity	100% Capacity
Machine hours	156,575	169,781	179,213	188,645
Approx. units	3,300,000	3,575,000	3,773,000	3,972,000
Period expenses:				
Factory	$5,346,000	$5,489,000	$5,489,000	$5,489,000
S and A	1,156,000	1,156,000	1,156,000	1,156,000
	$6,502,000	$6,645,000	$6,645,000	$6,645,000
Capital employed	$11,086,000	$11,413,000	$11,649,000	$11,886,000

Exhibit 7

The proportion of total period cost which can be reliably associated with a product line or other broad product classification is usually higher than is the proportion which can be associated with individual items in a line, or with individual job orders. For this reason, the assignment of period costs is often not carried beyond product lines. The marginal income ratio determined for the line is then used to establish a target ratio for pricing individual items in the line. The indicated selling price of any item can be readily calculated by dividing direct cost of the item by the complement of the marginal income ratio for the line. The same approach may be used to test alternative prices. To illustrate, the following hypothetical example demonstrates calculation of sales volumes needed to break even and to earn 20% on capital employed at selling prices which give marginal income ratios of 40% and 50% respectively.

Programmed period costs assigned to product:

Manufacturing	$ 40
Selling	25
Administration and General	5
Engineering	15
Other	5
Total Period Costs	$90

Capital employed

$1,000 at desired rate of 20%	200
Total marginal income required to cover period costs and provide a 20% return on capital employed	$290

	Marginal Income Ratio	
	40%	50%
Break-even sales volume (period costs ÷ marginal income ratio)	$225	$180
Sales goal (total period charges ÷ marginal income ratio)	$725	$580

Applying Different Mark-up Ratios to Material and Conversion Costs

The foregoing method may not give a satisfactory target price where individual products or orders differ markedly in their usage of common facilities. Under these conditions, it is preferable to compute the marginal income ratio in terms of some unit such as machine hours which measures equipment usage.

Individual products in a line may also differ with respect to relative proportions of material and conversion cost. In order to

	Profit Plan	Objective
Net sales (S)	$20,000	$20,400
Direct cost		
Material (M)	8,000	8,000
Labor & expense (L)	6,000	6,000
Total Direct Cost	14,000	14,000
Margin	6,000	6,400
P/V	30%	32.3%
Period expense	4,000	4,000
Net operating profit	2,000	2,400
% of (S)	10%	11.8%
Gross assets employed	12,000	12,000
% Return	16.7%	20%
S/M	2.50	2.55
L/M	.75	.75

Exhibit 8

obtain the same rate of return, it may here be necessary to apply different markup ratios to material cost and to conversion cost. Wilmer R. Wright has described the following method for developing pricing formulas for individual products in a line where the individual products have different proportions of material and conversion cost.[14]

"Take, for example, the XYZ Company . . . Product Line Y has a number of individual products which show a wide range of relative material content. Therefore, instead of dividing the direct cost of a product by the complement of the profit/volume ratio, the proper mark-up for material, as distinct from conversion cost, must be determined so as to give the same return regardless of relative material content.

"Exhibit 8 is illustrative. The present average return for Line

[14] "Direct Costs Are *Better* for Pricing," *N.A.A. Bulletin*, April 1960, pp. 17-26.

49

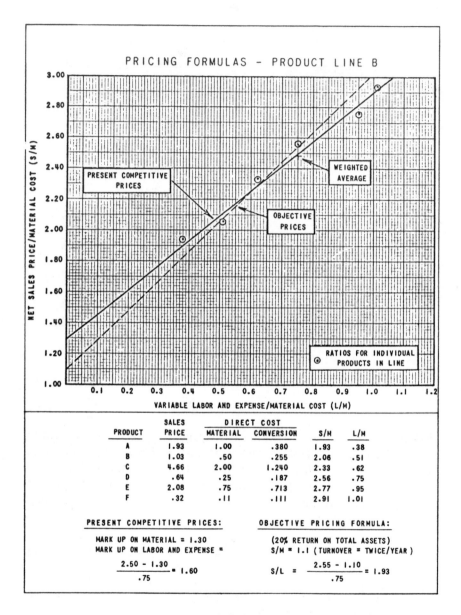

PRICING FORMULAS — PRODUCT LINE B

PRODUCT	SALES PRICE	DIRECT COST		S/M	L/M
		MATERIAL	CONVERSION		
A	1.93	1.00	.380	1.93	.38
B	1.03	.50	.255	2.06	.51
C	4.66	2.00	1.240	2.33	.62
D	.64	.25	.187	2.56	.75
E	2.08	.75	.713	2.77	.95
F	.32	.11	.111	2.91	1.01

PRESENT COMPETITIVE PRICES:

MARK UP ON MATERIAL = 1.30
MARK UP ON LABOR AND EXPENSE =

$$\frac{2.50 - 1.30}{.75} = 1.60$$

OBJECTIVE PRICING FORMULA:

(20% RETURN ON TOTAL ASSETS)
S/M = 1.1 (TURNOVER = TWICE/YEAR)

$$S/L = \frac{2.55 - 1.10}{.75} = 1.93$$

Exhibit 9

Y is 16.7 percent on capital employed. Assume that the pricing committee selects a 20 percent objective. By working back from the capital employed, it is easy to determine the objective margin ($6,400,000) and the objective sales income ($20,400,000).

"The mark-up on the material content is determined by the objective return and the turnover rate. In the case of Product Line Y, the turnover was found to be twice a year, so that a mark-up factor of 1.1 on the material content should produce a 20 percent return on capital employed. Thus the sales income that would be required to provide a 20 percent return on the capital employed in material ($8,000,000 multiplied by 1.10) is $8,800,000. The sales income required to provide a 20 percent return on capital employed in conversion is therefore ($20,400,000 less $8,800,000) $11,600,000. This, divided by the direct conversion cost gives the conversion mark-up factor ($11,600,000 ÷ $6,000,000 = 1.93).

"The formula for competitive prices is determined as follows: A group of products that are believed to be competitively priced are selected. A list is made showing for each product the sales price (S), the direct material cost (M), and the direct conversion cost (L). The ratios S/M and L/M are computed and a graph using S/M as the ordinate and L/M as the abscissa is drawn. The line of best fit is selected by visual inspection or the method of least squares. This line represents the competitive pricing formula, and the objective pricing formula is then drawn. Such a comparison of competitive practices with objective return on capital employed provides a clear understanding of areas in which improvements can be made within the competitive structure. Exhibit 9 shows this development for the XYZ Company."

Price figures determined by procedures described above are targets bearing a desired relationship to cost. In practice, management may consider it advisable or necessary to modify such target figures to reflect a variety of other factors such as customer demand and expected actions of competitors.

Measuring Relative Profitability of Segments

Some companies have little scope for independent action in setting selling prices. Typical situations are illustrated by comments such as those quoted below:

"This company follows prices set by industry leaders and is more concerned with what products to make than with how to price them."

"Price lines in this industry are firmly established by market custom and the company's fixed overhead is also established by the amount of capacity provided. The principal problems in pricing are how much direct cost is allowable (a matter largely determined by design of products) and how much volume can be obtained. Direct costing makes it easy to see how much can be spent for direct cost by price lines. It also facilitates subsequent control over the cost designed into a product because it provides for a positive check of actual costs against predesigned costs."

Other companies have a measure of control over their selling prices, but this control is limited by competition, either present or potential.

Under such circumstances it is important to know the relative profitability of products and also of other segments of the business such as markets and customers. Knowledge of relative profitability of the various segments helps management to decide which segments to emphasize, which ones need attention for profit improvement, and perhaps which ones can advantageously be replaced.

These segments are not independent of one another and cannot be evaluated separately to the point of net profit except by applying arbitrary methods of cost allocation which are not helpful in making decisions intended to improve sales mix by emphasizing the most profitable segments or by improving profitability of low margin segments. However, while it is not possible to determine the amount of net profit attributable to a given segment of business, it is possible to determine the rate at which one segment contributes to total profit from all segments combined. This rate is the marginal income figure. So long as period costs are not changed in total by pricing decisions, the period costs have no bearing on such decisions and need not be allocated to units being priced. On the other hand, marginal income is relevant to pricing decisions because direct costs and sales revenues do change with changes in selling prices and sales volume.

When marginal income is known, the amount of profit which will be added by an increment in sales can be determined without knowing the total profit from each product or other segment. Those segments which show the highest marginal income per unit will, of course, increase profit most rapidly as volume is increased. That is, for a product with a 40 percent marginal income ratio, each added dollar of sales increases overall net profit by 40 cents. For a product with a 20 percent marginal income ratio, each added dollar of sales adds only 20 cents to profits.

It is evident that aggregate profit can be increased if additional volume can be obtained for segments which carry high marginal income ratios. Hence added expenditures for advertising or perhaps price reductions will be profitable if they increase volume. With segments carrying low marginal income ratios, cost reductions or price increases are more likely ways to increase profit because here added volume alone adds little to profit.

Field interviews often pointed out that, for pricing decisions, marginal income should be computed in terms of the factor which limits the company's short-run output. For example, two products may have identical marginal income ratios per sales dollar or per physical product unit. However, if one of these products has to be processed at a slower speed and therefore occupies a larger fraction of available machine capacity, this product contributes less profit per machine hour. Unless the company's machine capacity exceeds the maximum volume of business obtainable, marginal income should be computed in terms of machine hours. In some cases, the factor which limits volume may be labor or materials rather than plant capacity. Thus one company reported that its capacity is limited by the size of its staff of experienced engineers and in pricing it endeavors to obtain the maximum marginal income per engineering man hour.

Evaluating Proposals to Increase Sales Volume

From time to time management in most companies considers proposals to increase sales volume by methods which reduce the unit net revenue realized from sales. These methods include spending more for advertising, expanding into markets where distribution costs are higher, offering additional services to the customer, or reducing selling prices. Also, where markets can be broken up into segments which do not compete with one another, it is common practice to sell at different prices or on terms which give different net sales realization. One company representative made the following comments on the usefulness of direct costing for guiding management in such pricing decisions:

> "Absorption costing tended to level out the effects of volume over months in the year and consequently obscured the effect of volume on profits. In our business, which is both seasonal and competitive, it was thought desirable to have management see clearly the monthly profit based on sales of the same month and also to show management that the cost of its products was tied to the volume sold—i.e., that there was no one unit cost figure so long as volume was a variable. They were then in a position to vary prices or take other action because they could predict what added volume would add to profits."

In some cases pricing decisions must be made promptly and opportunities are lost if decisions are delayed until costs can be analyzed. A company representative explained this problem as follows:

> "Our products are sold at variable prices. It is often necessary to make pricing decisions quickly—to take or to reject business

at an offered price. Direct costing makes it easy to ascertain what contribution such individual orders will make to total profit. As guides, we have a target contribution margin figure which has been calculated to recover fixed costs and give a target return on investment, and another figure at which the company breaks even, that is, recovers its costs without profit."

Company representatives generally agreed that the accountant has responsibility for making sure that a complete picture is presented to and understood by management. Thus when management considers acceptance of lower margin orders to increase volume, the accountant ascertains either that the added volume will not increase period costs by requiring expansion of plant, addition to salaried personnel, payment of overtime and shift premiums, or that such increased period costs have been included in cost of the orders under consideration. In addition, management should consider whether acceptance of a given order or class of orders may reduce the volume of more profitable business available at present or in the future.

While commonly viewed as a tool to aid in pricing to utilize capacity which would otherwise be idle, those who use direct costing feel that it is equally helpful in deciding what orders to accept when the volume of business available exceeds capacity. Under such conditions, the largest total net profit will result if those products are sold or those orders accepted which carry the highest rates of marginal income. As noted previously, marginal income needs to be stated in units of the factor which limits short-run capacity. However, a long-range view should be taken because actions which maximize profits in the short-run may not do so in the long-run. For example, to concentrate sales efforts on customers temporarily willing to pay the highest price will not be profitable in the long run if other customers are lost whose orders are needed to maintain volume during off-peak periods.

Understanding of Cost-Price Relationships

Most company representatives interviewed in this study expressed the opinion that direct costing had contributed toward better pricing by improving management's understanding of cost behavior. The following statement illustrates this point of view:

"Salesmen are very important members of this company's organization and have considerable authority to negotiate prices. They never could understand the absorption of overhead and how it varied by product lines. We have found they can understand

direct cost and contribution margins and they use this information very effectively in selective selling and pricing."

In other instances, it was stated that direct costing had made it
possible to show more clearly the profit consequences of pricing
decisions. Examples such as the following were often given
by company representatives:

When product costs include fixed overhead based on normal volume, management usually has only rough estimates to guide it in
deciding whether to meet competitive prices or to withdraw from
the market. Instances were cited in which management had un-
knowingly continued selling products below out-of-pocket cost or
had decided to withdraw from the market when a substantial portion of the period costs could have been recovered. Direct costing makes available cost data which enables management to make
such decisions with full knowledge of the effect these decisions
will have on profits.

In one interview, it was stated that sales management usually
questioned the allocations of period cost when products sold at competitive prices showed unsatisfactory profit margins over "full"
cost. When direct costing was introduced, analysis demonstrated
that contracts which would have contributed to period costs had
often been refused at times when the company had a large amount
of idle capacity.

In another company, the controller commented that, if period
cost were included in product costs, a number of the company's
products would appear to be unprofitable. Such figures might lead
management to drop the items showing a loss or to raise prices
of these items. In the controller's opinion, either action would
reduce total sales volume while leaving the same amount of period
cost to be spread over the smaller volume which remained. On
the other hand, with direct cost of the products available, management can see that so long as a product sells for more than its
direct cost, it should be retained until it can be replaced by a more
profitable item or its marginal income is less than the amount of
the period costs which can be eliminated by dropping the product.

Those who have not used direct costing often express fear that
direct costing will lead to underpricing and losses. For this reason, company representatives interviewed were questioned con-
cerning their companies' experience on this point. No instance
of unprofitable pricing attributable to direct costing was reported but, on the contrary, opinion was frequently expressd
to the effect that direct costing had contributed to better pricing
decisions. However, companies restrict product cost and margin
data to individuals qualified to interpret such data and responsible for pricing policy decisions. The following example illustrates this practice:

"Once a year when the budget is prepared fixed costs are distributed to operations and applied to products to obtain product costs for pricing. This is done because top management fears that sales personnel who make pricing decisions would price the company out of business if they were permitted to know contribution margins. The industry is characterized by cut-throat competition and many orders are taken below full cost, but decisions on such business are made only by the president and treasurer. They are the only persons who see profit contribution figures."

In general, it seems evident that consideration must be given to the understanding and judgment possessed by persons who make pricing decisions in each company. Absence of these characteristics in adequate measure can lead to unprofitable pricing regardless of the kind of cost data available or cost accounting system used. A number of the companies participating in this study have taken steps to educate personnel responsible for pricing in order to make sure that costing practices are understood. Following are two examples:

This company has a pricing department that established prices for its broad line of products. Members of this department sat in on discussions which took place when the company decided to adopt direct costing and they have a thorough knowledge of the company's costs. Moreover, they fully appreciate the necessity for obtaining prices high enough to recover period costs and to provide a profit on the stockholders' investment.

In another company, a sales department meeting is held every Monday morning to discuss subjects pertinent to the salesmen's work. From time to time the marginal income concept is presented by the use of basic examples. The company's sales personnel understand the relationship between cost and prices and are fully cognizant of what marginal income rates are needed to produce satisfactory operating results.

Summary

Selling prices seldom have a rigid relationship to product cost because competition and the elasticity of customer demand as well as cost enter into pricing decisions. Profits depend upon achieving a satisfactory combination of price, volume, and mix and for this reason volume needs to be viewed as a variable in assembling cost data to guide pricing.

Where market conditions allow independent action to be taken by a company in pricing its products, target prices are computed. Methods for arriving at mark-up factors applied to direct product cost are described in this chapter.

Where products must be sold at prices established in the market, the problem shifts to one of measuring the relative profitability of products or determining what kind of a product to produce. The marginal analysis provides the simplest approach to such questions because period costs which remain constant in total amount are irrelevant to the decision. Companies participating in this study report that direct costing has distinct usefulness to them in short-run pricing decisions.

chapter 5

THE ROLE OF DIRECT COSTING IN COST CONTROL

Costs are controlled by management actions directed at the sources from which the costs originate. The accountant's function in cost control is to supply data which enables management to act more effectively. These data are used both in the planning stage of control and in the review of performance where reports of current actual costs and analyses of variances are needed.

Underlying cost control reports are standards and budgets from which are determined the amount of cost allowable for the output attained. Companies using direct costing exclude period costs from overhead rates for costing production, but direct costing does not supplant standard costs for controlling direct costs and budgets for controlling period costs.

For the purpose of control, costs are accumulated and reported by control responsibilities established in the company's organization plan. While these are not unique features of direct costing, company representatives generally agreed that direct costing supports and facilitates the use of these accounting tools for cost control. In fact, improved cost control was a major objective of some of the companies participating in this study when they decided to adopt direct costing. This can be seen in the following statement made by one of these companies which, before conversion to direct costing, had employed standard costs incorporating allocations of period costs to products through cost center burden rates based on normal volume:

> "The broad general objectives to which this entire program was addressed were the identification and control of variable costs and their subsequent effect upon variable margin. In addition, we desired to develop a control program for our capacity costs. The program recognized the essential differences in control measures applied to variable vs. capacity costs."

This chapter aims only to point out the principal relationships between accounting tools of cost control and direct costing. Techniques such as standard costs and budgets have been described elsewere in accounting literature.[15]

Establishing Responsibility for Cost Control

Since costs are controlled by people with authority to make cost incurring decisions, costs should be budgeted and reported by control responsibilities established by the company's organization plan. In order that performance under each control responsibility may be clearly and objectively measured, costs which are not controlled by the responsible individual should be omitted or separated from costs which the individual is expected to control.

A number of company representatives interviewed commented that direct costing facilitates management by exception because the income statement and auxiliary schedules are more easily arranged to measure performance by responsibilities established in the company's organization plan. In additon, period costs are reported separately and therefore can be grouped by functional responsibility which is not obscured by distributions of non-controllable costs.

While the foregoing advantages apply at the departmental level, direct costing may also help to provide top management with a better picture of the company's period costs. In the words of a company representative:

> "Organization of the income statement to show the relationships between marginal income, period costs, and net income has emphasized the importance of controlling the period costs. By showing the totals of such costs, it is easy to observe upward trends."

In another case it was stated that direct costing provides continuing opportunity to review period costs in relation to the level of sales and net income. Management may be led to examine the benefits received from existing programs for plant maintenance, engineering, purchasing, sales promotion and similar functions that are sources of period costs. The effect on cost of any change in such programs is readily observed in the income statement.

Summary income statements are supplemented by auxiliary statements designed to bring to management's attention those items which constitute exceptions to plan. For example, when direct costing was adopted by a medium sized company which

---

[15] See, for example, *How Standard Costs are Being Used Currently*, Research Series Nos. 11-15; *The Analysis of Cost-Volume-Profit Relationships*, Research Series Nos. 16-18.

manufactures on a job lot basis, a marginal income rate of 45% was established as a target figure. Individual orders which show a marginal income ratio of less than 38% are listed on a report which goes to the president monthly. By scanning this list, he can quickly see what types of orders are falling below the company's profit goal, how large they are relative to total sales, and who quoted the price.

Separation of Direct and Period Costs in Cost Control

That the process of classifying costs into direct and period categories also helps to strengthen control over costs has been pointed out by Frederick J. Muth as follows:[16]

> "This separation brings an understanding of expense behavior to the production manager, the industrial engineer, and the sales manager, far beyond their experience in developing the flexible budget. The examination of an expense item for classification in the proper category forces investigation as to its actual need and amount. Expenses which have been accepted over the years as necessary at certain activity levels receive far more careful study before they are allowed because they are looked at in a new perspective."

Persons interviewed stated that top executives were sometimes astounded when they first learned the amount of period cost associated with being ready to do business. Under absorption costing it is possible for top management to lose sight of the individual period costs. For example, if costs of departments such as purchasing, industrial engineering, production control, timekeeping, payroll, receiving, and plant protection are worked into the manufacturing overhead rate, these costs are shown in the financial statements only as inventory and cost of goods sold.

The decisions needed to keep these costs under control must be made at the administrative rather than at the supervisory level of management. For this reason, many of the company representatives interviewed emphasized that the summary operating statement should be designed to show the full amounts of period administrative, clerical, and service expenses. Where direct costing is in use, these expenses are collected in period cost accounts and the totals can be reported in operating statements as shown in Exhibit 10. Supporting details by department and nature of expense are also readily available in the underlying accounts.

---

[16] An Evaluation of Direct Costing, *The Controller*, February 1957, p. 65.

Details		Operating Statement Showing Period Expenses by Functional Responsibilities				
	Actual	Budget	Variance favorable or (unfavorable)	Responsibility of	
				Name	Title
Sales	$3,100,000	$3,400,000			
Cost of sales (at std.)	1,922,000	2,040,000			
MARGINAL INCOME (at std.)	$1,178,000	$1,360,000	(182,000)	J. Smith	V. P. of Sales
Variations from standard					
On purchasing materials	5,000	-	5,000	T. Brown	V. P. of Pur.
On processing materials	(28,950)	-	(28,950)	W. Lowe	V. P. of Mfg.
MARGINAL INCOME (Actual)	$1,154,050	$1,360,000	(205,950)		
Period expenses:					
Manufacturing	$ 185,400	$ 182,000	(3,400)	W. Lowe	V. P. of Mfg.
Personnel	125,400	124,500	(900)	C. Downs	V. P. of Per.
Accounting	89,100	84,000	(5,100)	B. Brown	Controller
Marketing	90,175	82,000	(8,175)	J. Smith	Mgr. of Mkt.
Purchasing	67,800	62,900	(4,900)	T. Brown	V. P. of Pur.
Plant engineering	38,225	40,500	2,275	R. Roy	Dir. of Eng.
Legal	43,290	38,750	(4,540)	A Wiley	Secretary
Treasury	35,410	37,200	1,790	W. Cash	Treasurer
Public relations	25,200	26,800	1,600	D. Cole	Dir. of P. R.
Research & development	21,850	18,300	(3,550)	A. Mack	V. P. of Res.
Total period costs	$ 721,850	$ 696,950	(24,900)		
PROFIT BEFORE TAXES	$ 432,200	$ 663,050	(230,850)		

Exhibit 10

How Control of Period Costs Differs from Control of Direct Costs

The distinction between direct and period costs is an essential one to effective control of costs because the techniques and tools of control differ. Development of the amounts of direct and period costs by routine processes of recording and summarizing costs in the accounts is generally considered to be an advantage of direct costing in the area of cost control.

Unit cost standards are the principal accounting tools for controlling direct costs in the centers where these costs originate. These standards are expressed in terms of the unit of activity

Departmental Budget Report - Variable

Department or Cost Center:	Sm. Eng. & Turret Lathes		Budget Base: Dir. Labor Hrs.	
Supervisor:	J. Doe		Month of:	
Description	Expense Code	Actual	Budget	Variance
Paid lunch	02	$ 37	$ 97	$ 60
Direct labor	04	6 824	6 785	(39)
Indirect labor	05	226	779	553
Service labor	06	652	716	64
Rework	08	274	333	59
Instructors & learners	09		238	238
Misc. delays	10	618	462	(156)
Overtime premium	14	119		(119)
Social security taxes	15	211	455	244
Group insurance	17	414	346	(68)
Workmen's compensation	18	142	174	32
Repair & maintenance	60	1 098	1 302	204
Utilities	67	131	124	(7)
Operating supplies	70	1	127	126
Small tools	71	106	432	326
Defective product	78	994	1 582	588
Total		$11 847	$13 952	$2 105

Exhibit 11

Departmental Budget Report - Capacity

| Department or Cost Center: | Plant Occupancy | | Budget Base: Fixed | |
| Supervisor: | L. W. Smith | | Month of: | |
Description	Expense Code	Actual	Authorized Budget	Variance
Indirect labor	05	$ 2 996	$ 1 940	$ 1 056.
Vacation wages	13	185	153	32.
Overtime premium	14	85		85.
Social security taxes	15	81	112	31
Pensions	16	75	88	13
Group insurance	17	79	91	12
Workmen's compensation	18	32	36	4
Telephone & telegraph	35	2 147	2 259	112
Repair & maintenance	60	10 094	8 614	1 480.
Utilities	67	300	302	2
Operating supplies	70	1 347	1 400	53
Depreciation	80	2 853	2 735	118.
Lease expense	82	54		54.
Property tax	85	4 276	3 149	1 127.
Rentals	86	29	6	23.
Fire & liability insurance	88	1 828	1 453	375.
Total		$26 461	$22 338	$4 123.

Exhibit 12

(e.g. pieces or productive standard hours produced) which causes the amount of direct cost to vary. From these standards, the supervisor responsible can readily determine the amount of each direct cost allowable for the specific volume of production scheduled. Periodically, the accountant compares actual with allowed costs and reports variances. Exhibit 11 illustrates the form in which variable expense budget reports are prepared by one company.

On the other hand, the amount of period cost is independent of short-period fluctuations in activity. Period costs are accordingly budgeted for control as a specified number of dollars per month or per year. Management control proceeds by limiting the number of employees and the consumption of services to quantities which formed the basis for the period allowance budgeted. Variances reported by the accountant are measured by comparing actual expense for the period with the corresponding budget allowance. Exhibit 12 shows a departmental cost control statement for period costs.

Only a few of the companies participating in this study use step budgets for period or semi-variable costs. In a majority of cases it was stated that plant activity ordinarily does not vary enough to require that period expenses be budgeted in steps. However, variances from budget arise when substantial changes in activity do occur.

Where step-budgets are prepared, management wishes to be ready so that expense control does not lag when period costs should be adjusted. Company representatives also explained that step budgets have educational value in that they help supervisors to understand that period costs are fixed by management decisions that hold only within limited ranges of volume. Opinion was expressed to the effect that a more thorough study of expenses is required in order to set good step budgets.

Steps in expense budgets represent major activity levels that call for different amounts of period expense. An example of step budgeting appears in Exhibit 13.

For purposes of control, some companies separate period costs into groups. Thus one company distinguishes "committed costs" and "managed costs". The committed costs are fixed in the short-run by past decisions which entail continuing charges for depreciation, property taxes, rentals, and similar items. Managed costs include items controllable to a considerable extent by management judgment, but not proportionately variable with current volume of production and sales. Examples of managed costs

Capacity Cost Step Budgets

Dept. No.	Department	Planned Budget Base 63768 Hrs.	Step 1 50000 Hrs.	Step II 40000 Hrs.	Step III 30000 Hrs.	Step IV 20000 Hrs.
02	Occupancy	$ 44628	$ 43744	$ 43302	$ 42860	$ 37556
11	Production cont.	12489	11632	10204	9062	5349
13	Purchasing	13582	13117	11721	10325	5672
15	Cost & factory payroll	12968	11942	10146	8350	4502
28	Finished stores	6442	5798	5476	4510	2577
	All other depts.	183142	172329	158377	145778	98768
	Total	$273251	$258562	$239226	$220885	$154424

Exhibit 13

65

are advertising, executive and supervisory salaries, and staff services such as accounting, industrial relations, etc.

It was frequently reported that direct costing has simplified the task of budgeting overhead expense because inter-departmental distribution of period expenses is eliminated. This also eliminates the necessity for forecasting departmental volume as a base for overhead rates or, if expected volume differs from expense absorption volume, forecasting volume variances.

Several companies participating in the study use both departmental and plant-wide costing rates for direct overhead expense. Here departmental overhead rates include variable expense originating and controlled in individual departments. Plant-wide rates are developed for general expenses variable with production but not controlled by departmental supervisors. Expenses of the latter type include preventive maintenance, supplies not controlled by requisition procedures, and certain fringe benefits. Responsibility for control of such items rests with general plant management which establishes policies under which the expenses arise. However, the cost is applied to production through an hourly rate in each production department.

At the top management level, control is directed toward profit rather than toward costs alone. In the field study, it was repeatedly stated that top management's understanding of the factors influencing profits has improved since direct costing was introduced. This has, in turn, led to greater reliance on accounting reports by management personnel. Reasons given to explain why direct costing has had this effect are reported in Chapter 6.

Summary

Those who use direct costing generally agree that the separation of direct and period costs in the accounts and operating reports supports the use of standards, budgets, and responsibility reporting to aid management in controlling costs. The principal reason given for this is that the processes of accounting for costs under direct costing conform more closely to the requirements of cost control than they do where direct costing is not in use. Thus responsibility for control of period costs—particularly those in the "managed" category—rests with management at the administrative level. Direct costing causes these costs to be collected and reported in the income statement as separate deductions from marginal income instead of being merged with cost of goods sold and inventory. Where the latter practice prevails, the separate identity of manufacturing period costs and their impact on profits tends to be lost to view.

chapter 6

DIRECT COSTING IN FINANCIAL REPORTS TO MANAGEMENT

The measurement of net income for periods of time is a process of matching costs and revenues by fiscal periods. If the streams of costs and revenue both ran at a uniform rate through time, the timing of charges against revenues would raise no serious accounting questions. However, the flow of costs and revenues varies, often substantially, from period to period and the two streams are frequently not synchronized. In preparing periodic income statements, the accountant is accordingly faced with the problem of matching costs with the revenues to which the costs are relevant.

Function of Inventory in Measuring Periodic Income

Some costs are viewed as deferred charges to be matched with revenues in future periods while other costs are viewed as costs of the current period and hence not deferrable. Manufacturing costs are, when deferred, carried forward to future periods as inventory while other categories of cost carried forward (e.g. prepaid rent, taxes, insurance) are termed deferred charges or prepaid expenses.

Direct costing differs from absorption costing in that, under direct costing, period manufacturing costs are not deferred in inventory but are charged against the period in which the costs are incurred. That is, under direct costing, period costs of manufacturing are matched with revenues on a time basis rather than on a product unit basis. The only costs deferred in inventory are variable manufacturing costs of finished and unfinished goods on hand at the close of the period. This procedure makes it necessary to distinguish between direct and period manufacturing costs when the costs are recorded in the accounts.

When production and sales are in balance, net operating profit is the same under both direct and absorption costing. However, whenever the inventory of manufactured goods changes from one period to the next, the two methods give different profit figures. The reason for this difference is that the timing of charges against revenues is not the same under the two methods. For any two successive periods, the difference between profit determined by absorption costing and by direct costing is equal to the change in the amount of period cost deferred in inventory.[17]

The principal usefulness attributed to direct costing by its proponents arises from its application in forecasting and reporting income in a manner which shows clearly the relationships between cost, volume, and profit. While it has sometimes been described as a method for costing inventory, this feature is a means toward the end, which is measurement of income, and not an objective in itself. Likewise, the classification of costs into direct and period categories has other uses such as cost control, but this classification is integrated into the accounts primarily because the accountant wishes to distinguish between these two classes of costs in matching costs with revenues.

While few persons with an understanding of direct costing question its value for measuring income margins in profit planning and in making operating decisions, many accountants do question its acceptability for reporting periodic income in a company's historical financial reports. An attempt to appraise the usefulness of direct costing for measuring periodic income may proceed in two ways. First, analysis may be employed to determine whether or not the method is founded upon logical reasoning consistent with that underlying related techniques. Second, it may be tested by the practical usefulness of the results it produces in comparison with alternative methods. The latter test will be the ultimate one, for it may be expected that the method which has superior usefulness for the intended purpose will eventually gain acceptance as standard practice.

The remainder of this chapter examines direct costing for internal reporting of income to management. Chapter 7 takes up additional questions which arise when the use of direct costing is extended to external reports.

---

[17] For a fuller explanation and illustration of the manner in which this difference arises, see *Direct Costing*, Research Series No. 23, Chapter 5. This earlier report on direct costing also presents generalizations with respect to the size and direction of the divergence in periodic profit figures determined by the two methods.

Over the life of a business enterprise all costs incurred may be matched with all revenues received to determine net income. For determining life-time profit, the timing of charges and credits and the relevance of costs to revenues raises no questions. The actual quantity produced is the volume base for computing long-run average unit cost.[18] This situation is an extreme case useful chiefly for testing theory. Nevertheless, practical applications of long-run income measurement arise in making decisions regarding acquisition of long-lived assets. Here it is unnecessary to assign costs to interim periods in the life of the asset or to units of product and to do so may obscure the picture.[19]

In measuring periodic income, the accountant is, with few exceptions, dealing with periods shorter than the life of the enterprise, of depreciable assets used in the business, and of commitments made by management establishing costs which are independent of current volume fluctuations. Presence of these costs of maintaining capacity to do business is a distinguishing characteristic of the short-run income measurement problem, for in the long-run, there is no difference between direct and period costs. Similarly the time of charges against revenue is an important problem in measuring income for short periods.

Historical Evolution of Inventory Costing Techniques

Early in the development of cost accounting, physical inventories were often extended at unit prime cost and all other costs recognized during the period were charged off currently. With increased mechanization, manufacturing overhead became more important and the accountant sought techniques with which to include it in unit cost of the goods manufactured. The concept of unit cost adopted in accounting was that of a long-run unit cost.

However, difficulties were encountered in applying this long-run concept of unit cost for short-period determinations of product cost and profit. When unit cost was based on the actual monthly or annual volume of production, unit product costs tended to fluctuate inversely with volume. In periods of low volume, unit costs rose, perhaps above the price at which the goods could be sold. This effect came, of course, from using a short

---

[18] However, even in the long-run, costs of individual products are indeterminate where costs are jointly incurred for the several products.

[19] See Return on Capital as a Guide to Managerial Decisions, N.A.A. Research Report 35, Chapter 8.

Charging Production with Period Cost at Standard Unit Rate

Period	Production in units	Depreciation Annual amount	Cost Charged to production at standard Rate at 10¢ per unit	Volume variance dr (cr)	Sales in units	Cost of Sales Standard	Cost of Sales Actual
1	2	3	4	5	6	7	8
1	20,000	$ 2,000	$ 2,000		10,000	$ 1,000	$ 1,000
2	10,000	2,000	1,000	$1,000	10,000	1,000	2,000
3	30,000	2,000	3,000	(1,000)	40,000	4,000	3,000
4	10,000	2,000	1,000	1,000	20,000	2,000	3,000
5	30,000	2,000	3,000	(1,000)	20,000	2,000	1,000
	100,000	$10,000	$10,000	0	100,000	$10,000	$10,000

Exhibit 14

70

period volume base to implement a cost concept which called for a long-run volume base.

To avoid fluctuations in unit cost of production as a result of fluctuations in volume of production, the concept of a normal or standard volume per period was evolved. While defined in many ways, the basic idea of normal volume was that standard volume for each period should be a pro rata share of the ultimate long-run total. For example, if a machine has a useful life of five years and will produce 100,000 units during this period, the standard annual volume under this concept would be 20,000 units. The aim was to stabilize unit cost by replacing the fluctuating actual volume base with the concept of long-run cost. In practice it is likely to be a very crude approximation because accurate forecasts of long-range volume can rarely be made.

Standard Volume as Base for Costing Rates

By costing production at a standard unit rate based on standard volume, stable unit product costs are obtained and standard cost of sales is proportional to sales volume for the period. These characteristics are illustrated in Exhibit 14. The result is that unit fixed cost appears to behave exactly like unit variable cost—a fact which should not be unexpected since, in the long run, there are no fixed costs.

However, actual volume for short periods often differs from standard volume and fixed manufacturing costs are under or overabsorbed. The variable behavior of unit fixed cost of production can then be maintained only by carrying to a volume variance account the amount of fixed cost under or overabsorbed at the standard rate. This stabilized unit cost is thus a fiction rather than a reality.

If long-run volume could be accurately forecasted, periodic volume variances could be deferred with assurance that debits and credits would ultimately offset. Under such conditions, periodic cost of sales would vary directly and proportionately with volume of sales. For example, if annual volume variances shown in Column 5 of Exhibit 14 are carried forward as deferred debits or credits, the resulting annual cost of sales figures are those in Column 7.

Under extreme volume fluctuations, obviously absurd accounting results may result if period costs are deferred in inventory. G. J. Barry has described the following case[20]:

---

[20] "Continental Can's System of Financial Planning and Control", American Management Association Financial Management Series No. 108, p. 19.

". . . I can recall instances where some plants in our company have had an exceptionally heavy production schedule for a few months because it was necessary to build up inventories in anticipation of a seasonal pack of fruits or vegetables. During such months, the volume of production was many times greater than the sales volume. Prior to our use of the direct costing technique, the element of fixed cost was included in the standard cost which was used as the basis for charging inventory with the cost of production. When the actual monthly production was far in excess of one-twelfth of the annual production, we charged inventory with more fixed cost than was actually incurred and an overabsorption of cost resulted. In short, we were creating profit by producing for inventory. We even encountered instances where the amount of the monthly profit actually exceeded the amount of the month's sales. . . . An accounting system that produced a profit in excess of sales volume just didn't make sense to our operating executives. . . ."

In practice, volume variances are sometimes deferred during the year by companies whose operations have a quite regular seasonal pattern, but any underabsorbed balance remaining at the end of the year is virtually always written off. Overabsorbed balances are, if material in amount, usually apportioned between cost of sales and inventory. While some companies attempt to minimize volume variances by revising standard volume to expected actual volume at frequent intervals, this in effect approaches the practice of basing unit costs on current actual volume rather than upon long-range standard volume.

As a result, cost of sales tends to fluctuate without apparent relationship to volume of sales (see Exhibit 14, Column 8). The reason is that a second independent variable, i.e., volume of production, is introduced as a cause of fluctuations in cost of sales. Therefore, net income for a given period may be reduced by low production during that period (Exhibit 14, Periods 1 and 2) and increased by high production even though sales volume remains constant (Exhibit 14, Periods 4 and 5).

Information accumulated in N.A.A. research studies over a period of years indicates that the concept of a long-range normal or standard unit cost for costing production, sales, and inventory is not often applied in practice. The following reasons seem to explain failure to carry out theory based on the long run concept of cost:

1. Long-range normal or standard volume cannot be reliably determined. First, this is a consequence of the fact that long-range volume for a growing company with indefinite future life cannot be defined in concrete terms capable of being im-

72

plemented by measurement techniques. Second, long range forecasts of future volume have, at best, a wide and unknown margin of error. Lacking confidence in this standard, the accountant is unwilling to carry volume variances forward in the balance sheet because he knows that error in forecasting future volume could cause deferred period cost balances to grow rather than to offset.

2. The services of manufacturing facilities and organization tend to expire with passage of time whether or not utilized to produce salable goods. Consequently, the period costs of these services also expire with time. To carry such costs forward to future periods results in mismatching of costs with revenues because no benefits from such costs will be received in the future and nothing is contributed by the costs toward production of future revenues. Thus, the practice of charging unabsorbed period cost against revenues of the current period has been justified by reasoning that this charge measures cost of idle capacity and not cost of production. Similarly, apportionment of large overabsorbed balances reflects the opinion that unit production costs based on standard volume have been overstated.

While it seems to be generally agreed that costs of idle capacity should be treated as a current period charge,[21] practices commonly used for setting standard volume may cause undetermined amounts of idle capacity cost to be included in overhead rates employed for costing production. Thus when the standard volume base for overhead rates is revised from year to year to reflect experienced or expected volume, the cost absorption volume may be lower than the practical capacity. Period cost associated with this idle capacity is included in production cost.

Idle capacity cost is effectively eliminated from cost of production only where period cost absorption rates are based on practical productive capacity of the plant and changed only when changes in plant facilities cause changes in capacity. Information accumulated in a number of N.A.A. studies indicates that this practice is rarely followed.

The foregoing examination seems to lead to the conclusion that the concept of long-run unit cost of production is unsatisfactory in measuring short period income. The fault in this case is that the wrong cost concept was chosen for the purpose—i.e., the long-run concept of cost was used to measure short-run operations.

---

[21] See American Institute of Certified Public Accountants, Accounting Research Bulletin No. 43, Chapter 4.

Short-Run Cost for Short-Period Income Measurement

The concept of a short-run cost relates, not to a time period of specific length, but rather to any period shorter than the duration of commitments which establish period costs. The customary monthly, quarterly, and annual accounting periods are obviously interim periods in the life of manufacturing equipment and of policies with respect to maintenance of a basic organization.

Short-run unit cost should include only these costs which tend to be incurred by producing during the period in question and to be avoided by not producing. These are the costs which tend to vary directly and proportionately with volume of production. Those costs which remain the same in total—i.e., the period costs —should be excluded from short-run unit cost. Short-run costs have the following characteristics which are significant in measuring periodic income:

1. Unit direct or variable cost of production is objectively measurable because the amount of such cost tends to vary directly and proportionally with volume of production. On the other hand the amount of period cost is independent of the volume of production within limits for which capacity provided remains the same. Therefore, period costs can be attached to product units only by making an arbitrary assumption as to the volume of production over which to spread the period costs.

2. Benefits acquired by incurrence of direct costs expire with sale of the related goods. Having once been incurred to produce goods, direct costs need not be incurred again until more goods are produced. In other words, by producing goods in the current period the amount of direct cost which must be incurred in future periods is reduced in proportion to the direct cost of the goods carried forward. For this reason, the direct cost of goods on hand is deferrable as inventory until the benefits expire by sale of the goods. In contrast, the amount of period cost to be incurred in future periods cannot be reduced by producing goods to be carried forward in inventory, nor can the current period costs be reduced by producing less in the current period.

Under direct costing, the first step in measuring income for a period is to deduct direct costs from revenues recognized during the period. Consistency in the concepts of cost and income used is maintained, for short period revenues are matched with related short run costs. Direct costs which have been incurred to produce goods remaining on hand at the end of the period are carried forward as inventory. The short-run marginal income which results from this matching process is relevant to the various types of short-run decisions described in earlier chapters of this report. Gross income, as determined by absorption costing methods, is not relevant to these purposes because it is not based upon the consistent short-run concepts of both cost and income.

Period costs are, of course, excluded from marginal income. Over a series of short periods cumulative marginal income should be adequate to cover period costs plus a return on investment, although the amount of long-run net income cannot be determined with certainty until the enterprise has been liquidated. However, stockholders are unwilling to wait for a long period before learning how much, if any, profit has been made. Instead, they wish to know, from time to time, the rate at which long-run net income is being earned and they also wish to receive dividends and higher market values for their shares as the income is earned. Management likewise is interested in knowing at frequent intervals how successful it has been in achieving long-run profit goals. By giving recognition to the distinction between the short run and the long run concepts of cost, it is possible to show in the same income statement, both short run income for the current period and the same period's share of long run income.

Matching Period Costs With Current Revenue

The problem of determining what portion of long run cost to match with revenues of each month, quarter, and year centers upon the period costs. The accountant begins by assigning period costs to periods of time. Many of these costs (e.g. depreciation) are common to several periods. While the choice of a basis for allocation to periods can be rationalized, it is impossible to defend any one basis as correct to the exclusion of all other bases that might be used. For example, the percentage-of-declining-balance depreciation method may give annual depreciation costs which have certain advantages (e.g. tax savings) in comparison with the straight-line method, but it cannot be shown that any method gives the correct annual depreciation cost.[22]. In the ab-

---

[22] The situation is essentially the same as that where several products are produced jointly from a common raw material. Here the products have no objectively determinable separate costs, although arbitrary allocations of the joint cost can be made. Similarly, when a machine is purchased, a lump sum cost is incurred for several years' capacity or a number of units of future production. This cost is joint as to years and units and can be separated only by some subjectively chosen method. Such a method must include a forecast of the future life or production of the machine as well as a decision as to how the cost is to be apportioned among periods or units. (See also Research Series No. 31, *Costing Joint Products*, and Research Series No. 33, *Current Practice in Accounting for Depreciation*.)

sence of other criteria, period costs are usually spread equally over periods of time unless practical considerations such as tax advantages call for some other plan of allocation.

When period costs have been assigned to periods there remains the question as to whether these period costs of manufacturing should be matched with revenues on a time basis or on a product unit basis.

1. Absorption costing spreads period manufacturing costs over production of the period by using a common unit for measuring production (e.g. direct labor hours) and a chosen volume of production. Costs so applied to products are carried in inventory until the products are sold, at which time the costs are matched with revenues. Other period costs (e.g. underabsorbed manufacturing overhead, selling costs, general administrative costs) are charged in total against revenues of the period.

2. Direct costing deducts the total period cost from marginal income of the same period. The effect is to match period costs with revenues of the same period.

In determining short-run income for short-run decision making, analytical thinking clearly leads to the conclusion that marginal income is the concept of income relevant to the purpose and experience seems to show that direct costing is a useful technique to implement the concept.

The theoretical support cannot be equally strong for any method of measuring net income for short periods because all methods unavoidably rest upon more or less arbitrary assignments of long run period costs to short periods of time. However, these methods are based upon recognition that period costs are incurred to provide capacity and that opportunity to use this capacity tends to expire with passage of time regardless of whether it is used or not used. Thus buildings and machines grow obsolete and suffer physical deterioration with age; time of employees passes; and services such as insurance also expire. Since the benefits expire independently of use, the fact that some of the period costs are related to facilities used to manufacture goods which are on hand at the end of the period seems irrelevant to the matching process. The same costs will have to be incurred over again in future periods if the same capacity is maintained and the future amount of this cost is not diminished by possession of an inventory of goods manufactured earlier. Such reasoning supports the matching of period costs with revenues on a time basis rather than on a unit basis.

The opposite point of view is that cost of manufacturing capacity expires with time only when not utilized. To the extent that this capacity is employed to produce goods saleable in the future, cost of capacity is attached to the goods and matched with revenues when the goods are sold. The cost accounting processes whereby period costs are attached to the goods require decisions as to the unit in which to measure production and the volume over which the costs are spread. In multi-product plants, period costs are often joint as to several products and no fully satisfactory basis for allocation can be found. Since the processes of allocating fixed costs to periods and to product units require arbitrary decisions, it cannot be proved that one method is correct and another incorrect.

Practical Usefulness of Direct Costing for Measuring Income

The pragmatic test of comparative usefulness of direct and absorption costing remains. The remainder of this chapter reviews experience and opinion regarding the use of direct costing for measurement of periodic income.

Experience of all but a few of the fifty companies participating in this study has led them to conclude that the income statement is more meaningful and more useful to management when presented in direct costing form. This added usefulness stems in part from the organization of detail in the direct costing statement and in part from the behavior of marginal income and net profit under conditions of fluctuating volume.

Organization of Data Shown in Income Statement

Proponents of direct costing usually view the arrangement of revenue, cost, and income margin data in the direct costing income statement as a major advantage derived from direct costing. In the course of the study, company representatives frequently stated that better communication with resultant improved understanding of cost-volume-profit relationships by management personnel is an important feature of direct costing.

Opinion was also expressed to the effect that income statements in the direct costing form are particularly useful in reporting operating results for individual segments of the total business such as products, sales territories, customers, etc. Management's principal purpose in using income statements for such segments is to judge performance of individual segments rela-

Job Order Cost Sheet

Cost Estimate: 4 - #22 Steam Boilers   Approved By

Prepared: Dec. 4, 1959   Present Oper. Level:

By: Thomas C. Jones, Sales Engineer   Sales Backlog:

Cost Elements	Estimated Cost Details	Amount
Material		
Raw	Bill of mtl. attached	$ 40,000
Stock parts	do.	20,605
		$ 60,605
Direct Labor		
Project engineering	1,800 hrs. @ $5.00	$ 9,000
Shop	11,000 hrs. @ $2.40	26,400
Field (erection on site)	700 hrs. @ $3.50	2,150
		$ 37,550
Variable Expenses		
Shop	70% of Shop labor	$ 18,480
Field	30% of Field labor	645
Freight	18,000 @ $.04	720
Commission	5% of Sales price	10,000
		$ 29,845
Total Out - Of-Pocket Cost		$128,000
Period Expenses & Profit		
Factory	$2 per hr. of Shop labor	$ 22,000
Adm. and general	10% of Sales price	20,000
Profit	15% of Sales price	30,000
		$ 72,000
	Bid price	$200,000

Exhibit 15

Job Order Cost Sheet		

J. H. Smith _____   Customer: Acme Mfg.

65% of capacity _____   Promised: 5/8/60

Approx. 6 wks. work _____   Completed: 5/15/60

Actual Cost		Over (under) estimate
Details	Amount	
Invoices & req.	$ 40,098	98
Stock requisitions	18,116	(2,489)
	$ 68,214	(2,391)
2,000 hrs. @ $5.00	$ 10,000	$ 1,000
11,940 hrs. @ $2.45	29,243	2,843
800 hrs. @ $3.60	2,880	730
	$ 42,123	$ 4,573
70% of Shop labor	$ 20,470	$ 1,990
30% of Field labor	864	219
18,432 @ $.04	737	17
5% of Sales price	10,000	-
	$ 32,071	$ 2,226
	$132,408	$ 2,226
Margin	$ 67,592	$ 4,408

Bid Data		
Lowest bid		$200,000
Name of company		Ours
Our bid		-
Pct. lowest bid under ours		-

Exhibit 15—(Cont'd)

tive to each other or relative to pre-established profit goals.[23] For this purpose, marginal income has a simple and easily understood meaning. It is the number of dollars by which presence of the segment increased total net income from all segments combined. Conversely, had a specific segment not been present, total net income would have been less by the amount of marginal income from this segment.

The explanation of individual segment gross or net income as determined by absorption costing is not simple and determining what total net income would have been in absence of the segment often requires reworking of cost data by skilled accountants. The following illustration presents the experience of a company participating in the field study:

> During a period when this company had considerable idle capacity, it was the successful bidder for a government contract. At completion of the work, costs assigned to the contract by the company's absorption costing system exceeded the selling price. In order to determine whether or not the company had benefited from accepting the contract, management had the job re-costed on an out-of-pocket basis. This showed that the contract had contributed something toward period costs which otherwise would have been unrecovered. Following this experience, management decided that it would be advantageous to have similar information for all jobs, both to guide bidding for orders and to measure the actual contribution to profit made by individual contracts. The job cost sheet illustrated in Exhibit 15 was therefore designed for the purpose. It will be noted that the estimate column on the cost sheet includes the amount of period expense and profit included in the bid price. Actual direct costs charged to the job are recorded in order that variances from estimate can be reviewed. However, it was decided that no purpose would be served by reviewing period costs in connection with each job completed.

There is usually a substantial amount of period cost which is common to the various segments and, under absorption costing, both gross and net income figures are heavily influenced by subjective judgments in selecting bases for allocating period costs. On the other hand, marginal income constitutes a more objectively determinable measure of performance than does gross income. By deducting from marginal income those period costs which are specific to each product or other segment, the contributions made to general cost and net profit can also be measured. If desired, common period costs can be allocated as a last step. In this way, costs which can be assigned with high precision are not mixed with costs which cannot be assigned with precision.

[23] Applications of direct costing for evaluating alternatives in profit planning were described in Chapter 3.

The practice of bringing together the period costs is considered particularly advantageous because management is able to see clearly the amount of such costs and the impact they have had on profits. From such an arrangement of income statement data, the company's break-even volume and margin of safety above the break-even volume are also evident. Opinion was frequently expressed to the effect that these figures are more effectively communicated to management through the income statement than they are when presented as supplementary statistics. One reason is that an understanding of the relationship between these statistics and the income statement requires considerable knowledge of accounting technique when the income statement is presented in absorption costing form.

Advantages Attributed to Direct Costing as a Method for Measuring Net Income

Under direct costing, periodic net income tends to follow sales volume and is not affected by changes in the inventory of manufactured goods. For this reason, direct costing was first described as a technique for preparing income statements that were more understandable and more useful to management.[24] Discussion in field interviews showed that this feature of direct costing is considered advantageous in most of the fifty companies covered by the study. Moreover, in the few cases where it is not considered to be an advantage, inventories of manufactured goods have usually been either so small or so stable that they have had little influence on changes in profits from period to period.

In the field interviews it was commonly stated that executives find income statements prepared in direct costing form to be more useful because sales volume changes can be traced directly to net income. As a period progresses, management makes decisions with the expectation that its decisions will have specific effects on profits. The historic income statement serves an important function in that it enables executives to check their impressions and expectations with the actual results. Thus if an increase in sales volume has been obtained and current operating reports show that control over selling prices and production costs has been maintained, management expects the increased volume to be reflected in increased profits. While this relationship between sales volume and profits is evident in the direct

---

[24] The first published description of direct costing stressed this point of view. See Jonathan N. Harris, "What Did We Earn Last Month?," *N.A.(C.)A. Bulletin,* Jan. 15, 1936.

costing income statement, absorption costing may cause it to be obscured by changes in the fixed cost component of inventory.

Accountants interviewed in the field study agreed that very few persons in management who receive periodic income statements understand the influence which changes in the fixed cost content of inventory have on profits reported by absorption costing. It was frequently stated that in those cases where profit determined by direct costing is converted to an absorption costing basis by an adjustment placed at the bottom of the statement, management generally relies upon the figure obtained by direct costing and disregards the adjustment.

In the course of the field study, company representatives described several instances in which management had been led to make erroneous decisions by reliance upon profit figures determined by absorption costing. These cases are briefly described below:

1. A company had experienced a steadily increasing volume of sales for a number of years preceding the brief recession that began in 1958. Plant capacity and inventories had been increased with expanding sales. When sales dropped and forecasts indicated that the upward trend in sales would not be resumed for at least several months, management decided that the inventory was larger than needed to support current sales. It therefore proposed that inventory be reduced and that the cash released be applied to reduce bank loans. However, when the impact that the inventory reduction would have on profits was determined, management decided against any inventory reduction. One of the company's accounting executives expressed opinion to the effect that profits had been overstated by accumulating fixed costs in inventory during the years of inventory build-up. While it was agreed that inventory reduction was desirable, management was unwilling to accept the lower profits which would accompany writing off a portion of the accumulated fixed cost.

2. Several companies reported that division managers had sometimes failed to cut-back production promptly enough when sales declined because they did not wish to accept the consequent reduction in profit. In one of these companies it was stated that direct costing has helped to avoid excessive inventory accumulation and losses from obsolescence by making clear the fact that goods have to be sold as well as manufactured before any profit is realized. Commenting on this aspect of direct costing, one individual stated that "it is to the interest of a general manager of a profit center to put goods into inventory with an absorption system because this will give him a profit on the amount of fixed costs put into inventory and increase his share when he is on a profit sharing basis. With direct costing there is no such incentive and a

manager will not be in the position of having to make decisions which are contrary to his own best interests."

3. In another case, the president had once received a monthly income statement showing a substantial net operating loss and, desiring to avoid further loss, he ordered the plant shut down until the cause of the loss could be found and corrected. A check of the pricing of sales orders and of factory costs disclosed no source of loss. Eventually, it was concluded that heavy shipments to customers during the month and the accompanying liquidation of fixed costs previously accumulated in inventory, combined with low production, had been responsible for the loss. In the meantime, production was lost for a number of days.

Opponents of direct costing point out, with truth, that such cases represent faulty interpretations rather than inherent faults in absorption costing. However, to the extent that direct costing makes it easier for management to understand the income statement, erroneous decisions based on misunderstanding are less likely to occur.

A number of companies reported that direct costing has made it possible to prepare monthly estimates of profits within a matter of hours after tabulation of sales for the period has been completed. This is possible because it is not necessary to determine the amount of manufacturing period expense absorbed in inventory and the amount chargeable to cost of sales. In one company visited, net income is estimated weekly by product lines. Each Monday morning the standard marginal income rate is applied to sales of the previous week to determine marginal income. A pro-rata weekly share of the annual budgeted period expense is then deducted from marginal income. These weekly estimates have been sufficiently accurate to keep management informed of profit trends.

Several companies also utilize direct costing in forecasting future profits from shipments on orders received. For example, in one organization a profit estimate is prepared at the beginning of each month. This is done by costing at standard direct cost the products which are scheduled to be shipped and deducting the month's budgeted period expenses. Along the same line another company keeps a running record of the marginal income contained in its sales backlog. Through doing this, management is able to observe whether the orders on hand are up to the organization's profit objectives and, at the same time, to obtain a preview of the company's future profits.

It was often reported that less analysis is needed to explain financial statements because cost-volume-profit relationships are evident in the income statement where direct costing is in use. This feature saves time executives would have spent studying supplementary explanatory material in order to understand what has happened.

Cases in Which Direct Costing Has Been Abandoned

N.A.A. research studies carried on over a period of years have yielded considerable information about cost systems used by several hundred companies. Review of this information showed four cases in which direct costing has been partially or completely abandoned.

Two companies abandoned direct costing systems when the companies were acquired by parent companies which did not use direct costing. In both cases parent companies required the newly acquired subsidiaries to adopt accounting procedures prescribed as standard by the parent. However, one of these companies continued to use some of the features of direct costing because local management was reluctant to do without reports it had found useful. This was the only one of the four cases in which management made extensive use of accounting data to guide decisions on internal operations.

In a third case, the company's initial accounting system had been set up by accountants from the parent company which used direct costing. However, management of the subsidiary had little understanding of direct costing and the system was probably not well designed to supply data for decision making purposes. When local management acquired more independence, the accounting system was revised and direct costing was eliminated. Interviewed two years later, accounting personnel stated that management still made little internal use of accounting data.

In the fourth case, both standard costs and direct costing were replaced by a simplified process costing system meeting only minimum requirements for external financial reports. The reason given was that management made virtually no use of accounting data.

Summary

Companies participating in this study generally feel that direct costing's major field of usefulness is in forecasting and reporting income for internal management purposes. The distinctive feature of direct costing which makes it useful for this purpose is the manner in which costs are matched with revenues.

In this chapter, advantages reported in the field study are stated and theory is developed to explain why these advantages are a logical consequence of the direct costing method of income measurement.

The marginal income figure which results from the first step in matching costs and revenues in the direct costing income statement is reported to be a particularly useful figure to management because it can be readily projected to measure increments in net income which accompany increments in sales. The theory underlying this observed usefulness of the marginal income figure in decision making rests upon the fact that, within a limited volume range, period costs tend to remain constant in total when volume changes occur. Under such conditions, only the direct costs are relevant in costing increments in volume.

The practical advantages attributed to the direct costing approach to the determination of net income are less closely related to the theoretical justification for the method than is the case for marginal income. Nevertheless, the benefits reported flow from the method followed.

The tendency of net income to fluctuate directly with sales volume was reported to be an important practical advantage possessed by the direct costing approach to income determination because it enables management to trace changes in sales to their consequence in net income. Another advantage attributed to the direct costing income statement was that management has a better understanding of the impact that period costs have on profits when such costs are brought together in a single group.

chapter 7

DIRECT COSTING IN EXTERNAL
FINANCIAL REPORTS

In preparing internal financial reports to be used solely by management, a company is free to use whatever methods of accounting it finds most useful for the purpose. On the other hand, in reporting to persons outside the management group, accounting methods employed must conform to standards accepted or required in reporting to such groups. Whether or not direct costing can be used in preparing external financial reports depends upon its conformance or nonconformance with standards applicable to such reports.

Financial reports are, of course, used by different persons for different purposes. For discussion here, three groups are recognized, namely, (1) stockholders, (2) creditors, and (3) federal income tax administrators. The first two groups are considered in this chapter and the tax status of direct costing is discussed in Chapter 8. The interests of others not included in the above groups (e.g. investment analysts, employees, economists) are probably like interests of stockholders in most respects.

Standards Applicable to Financial Reports for Stockholders

Periodic net income is the key figure in appraisal of the stockholder's investment in a company's shares. For this reason, the stockholder's primary interest is in the income statement. Since shares of many companies are actively traded in the securities markets, periodic net income figures should be as reliable as possible because these figures influence values currently placed on the shares by buyers and sellers.

The Inventory as a Deferred Charge Against Future Income

Direct costing has been opposed on grounds that it "understates" or "undervalues" the inventory. Before discussing this question, it is essential to have clearly in mind the concept of inventory which is generally accepted in accounting.

From the accountant's point of view, the inventory is a deferred charge against future revenues. This deferred charge consists of costs assigned to goods which are held for sale in future periods. Hence the question of whether or not period manufacturing costs should be included in inventory is not a question of whether or not such costs add value to the inventory because inventory costing is not a valuation process. Instead, the real question is what costs incurred in past periods should be deferred and matched with revenues of future periods. Under absorption costing, period manufacturing costs "absorbed" by goods on hand at the close of the period are deferred by inclusion in cost of the inventory. Under direct costing, period manufacturing costs are not deferred.

The reasoning underlying the two methods was stated in Chapter 6. There it was pointed out that absorption costing uses a long-run concept of product cost for costing inventory. Practical difficulties inherent in measuring long-run unit cost were described. It was also stated that the matching of long-run cost with short-period revenue constitutes an inconsistency in concepts. Only short-run costs are relevant to short-run revenues and marginal income is the only short-period income margin that can be determined without arbitrary allocations of cost to periods and units. Since expiration of benefits provided by period costs is more closely related to time than to production, it seems realistic to match period costs against revenues of the same period. The preceding chapter also presented evidence from the field study showing that users of direct costing believe that direct costing gives periodic net income figures that are more useful to management. There seems to be no reason why the same figures are not also more useful to stockholders.

It remains to be asked whether or not the direct costing concept of net income and the associated practice of stating inventory at direct cost meet currently accepted standards for reporting income to stockholders. The answer to this question cannot be definite because the standards are broad and leave scope for a wide range of individual interpretation.

A statement issued in 1947 by the American Institute of Certified Public Accountants' Committee on Accounting Procedure is often cited as an opinion to the effect that direct costing is not an acceptable practice in external income reporting.[25] How-

---

[25] Accounting Research Bulletin No. 43, Chapter 4.

ever, careful reading of the statement does not seem to bear out this impression. Beyond stating that "the exclusion of all overheads from inventory costs does not constitute an accepted accounting procedure," the opinion gives no specific indication with respect to what expenditures and charges are considered applicable to inventories. That direct costing was not considered in the statement is not surprising because very few accountants were then acquainted with the technique.

A substantial proportion of the accountants with whom the question was discussed in the course of this study expressed the opinion that the statement can reasonably be interpreted to include direct costing as an accepted procedure. Moreover, while 17 of the 50 companies participating in the study report to stockholders on a direct costing basis, in none of these cases had auditors given a qualified opinion or taken exception to the practice.

A more definitely worded opinion is contained in a statement of *Accounting and Reporting Standards for Corporate Financial Statements 1957 Revision* by the American Accounting Association's Committee on Concepts and Standards Underlying Corporate Financial Statements. The relevant lines from this statement read as follows:[26]

> ". . . the cost of a manufactured product is the sum of the acquisition costs reasonably traceable to that product and should include both direct and indirect factors. The omission of any element of manufacturing cost is not acceptable."

However, two of the seven members of the committee dissented from this definition of product cost on grounds that it denied the acceptability of direct costing in published financial reports. The statement explains reasons for these dissenting points of view in the following words.[27]

> "Direct costing does not exclude from product inventories those manufacturing costs directly attributable to current production, that is, varying with changes in the rate of manufacturing operations; it does exclude fixed manufacturing costs, on the ground that such invariant elements (like general administrative expenses) ought to appear as expense of the period in which they are incurred."

Conclusions derived from this dissent are quoted below:

> "They therefore conclude that direct costing is at least as acceptable in accounting theory as is the conventional (full costing) concept. Moreover, they believe that the use of direct costing procedures will, in many cases, yield results more useful to investors as well as to management."

---

[26] Page 4.
[27] Page 10.

88

Neither of the foregoing committee statements disclose any evidence which was examined or any reasoning which led to the conclusions stated. Consequently, the statements remain as unsupported opinions which offer little guidance to the accountant who seeks to arrive at a judgment of his own as to acceptability of direct costing in reporting to stockholders.

As can be seen from the statements quoted above, standards which are intended to guide decisions with respect to costs to be inventoried are broadly stated and conformance with such standards requires the accountant to decide what expenditures for manufacturing are "applicable" or "reasonably traceable" to products. As might be expected, the range of variation in practice is wide and many companies that do not use direct costing nevertheless exclude important items of fixed cost (especially depreciation, property taxes, insurance) from inventory. Such practices follow no reasoned plan of cost classification, but rather reflect a variety of motives such as conservatism, tax saving, placement of responsibility for costs, bookkeeping convenience, etc. Moreover, the use of LIFO may affect inventory cost and net income more drastically than does direct costing. On the other hand, as noted in Chapter 6, inventory often includes some idle capacity cost. Review of practice therefore seems not to disclose existence of any widely used standards which can be used to test acceptability of direct cost for costing inventory.

Direct costing is, of course, not widely used at present. That it would be so used is hardly to be expected in view of the fact that it was little known among accountants until very recently. Moreover, in addition to reluctance to change established methods, practical obstacles have often been encountered by companies that wished to use direct costing in preparing external financial reports. These obstacles are discussed in the last section of this chapter.

Nevertheless, evidence from various sources—accounting conferences, recent publications, and field interviews in this study— seems to indicate that interest in direct costing to supply management with financial data for decision making purposes is spreading rapidly. Experience of companies participating in this study also suggests that many of these companies will eventually wish to bring external financial reports into conformity with internal accounting procedures.

Direct Costing in Financial Reports to Long-Term Creditors

Long-term creditors look principally to the debtor's earning ability rather than to assets for assurance that interest payments can be made and loans eventually repaid. For this reason, the uses made of financial reports by long-term creditors are much the same as those made by stockholders.

However, banks, insurance companies, and other large creditors usually receive more detailed financial statements than do stockholders in those cases where shares are widely dispersed among holders who are not active in management. To present both profit projections and periodic financial statements in direct costing form would seem to be advantageous both to the company and to creditors. Such statements show the spread between direct costs and revenues, the amount of continuing fixed costs to be met, and the borrower's break even volume. Such information is useful to the creditor in appraising the earning potential of a company to whom he has made loans. The borrower with a favorable earning position should also find it easier to present the facts about his earnings and financial condition to creditors.

Direct Costing in Financial Reports to Short-Term Creditors

Short-term creditors such as banks and vendors are inclined to be working capital minded in that they watch carefully the current assets and their relationship to current liabilities. Such creditors usually are particularly interested in the inventory because the borrower often relies upon proceeds from turnover of the inventory to pay his short-term obligations.

Reflection on the significance of inventories in judging the strength of a borrower's financial position leads to the conclusion that cost of an inventory is less important than anticipated sales realization. In other words, the creditor's security is measured not by the amount of cost incurred, but by the number of dollars that will be available for paying debts after the inventory is sold. Cash realization from sales is, of course, not affected by accounting procedures which assign more or less cost to the inventory for the purpose of measuring periodic income.

However, cost of inventory is shown in statements certified by independent accountants and in practice this cost is a factor which guides lenders in deciding how much credit to extend.

However, only one of the companies participating in this study stated that the effect of direct costing on reported working capital had been a significant consideration in obtaining short-term credit. In this one case, the company's principal asset was its inventory of contract work in progress and, since the ratio of fixed expense to total cost was high, current liabilities would have exceeded current assets if inventory had been stated at direct cost.

The creditor's security is not, however, improved by accounting practices which increase the stated cost of the inventory. On the other hand, information as to probable realizable value of the inventory is highly relevant to the creditors' purpose and also should guide management in deciding how much it can borrow with safety. Where goods are manufactured to the customer's order, sales contracts covering specific goods in inventory may permit quite accurate determination of sales realization.

Practice in Use of Direct Costing for External Reporting

Practices followed in costing inventory by the fifty companies participating in this study are summarized in Exhibit 16. While all of these companies use direct costing for internal purposes, twenty-four convert inventories to a full absorption cost basis in financial statements released to stockholders and others outside the management group. Five other companies add some, but not all, period manufacturing expenses to inventory in external reports. The principal reasons why these companies continue to prepare external financial statements on an absorption cost basis are listed below:

1. Acceptance of direct costing as a method for determining income subject to federal income tax has not been obtainable in most cases. Some companies are reluctant to introduce differences between accounting methods used for tax purposes and for public financial reports. Also, where conversion to direct costing would involve a substantial write-off of period costs in inventory, management does not wish to accept this deduction from revenues unreduced by tax saving.

2. While it is usually agreed that direct costing can be useful internally, in the opinion of many accountants direct costing does not conform to accepted standards for external reporting. The field study suggests that this opinion is more strongly held by accountants in public practice than it is by accountants in industry.

3. In some cases, only certain subsidiaries or divisions of a com-

pany use direct costing. Financial reports of these organizational units are adjusted to absorption costing before consolidation.

In cases where external financial statements are converted to an absorption costing basis, company representatives frequently expressed the opinion that it would be preferable to report on a direct costing basis, but that practical difficulties had prevented doing so. These difficulties generally had their source in expected unfavorable reaction to direct costing by the auditors, disinclination by management to accept the initial write-off of period costs in inventories, and unwillingness of federal tax authorities to give permission for the change in accounting method. It was frequently stated that if acceptance for tax purposes could be obtained, the other obstacles would no longer be serious deterrents.

Introducing Direct Costing for External Reporting

Among the twenty-one companies participating in this study which exclude all period expense from inventories in external financial reports, there are several companies that have followed this practice consistently since organization of the company. Most of these early cost systems were not direct costing plans, for they limited the costs included in inventory for reasons of conservatism or to simplify accounting for costs. While a few companies in this group continue to cost inventories at prime cost, others revised manufacturing cost classifications when direct costing was introduced. However, since there was no important change in unit cost of inventory, no serious problems were encountered when direct costing was adopted.

On the other hand, others of the twenty-one companies now reporting on a direct costing basis formerly used absorption costing systems. A few of these companies found that product costs were not materially changed by the reclassification and revision of costs undertaken when direct costing was introduced. For example, in some cases certain direct costs previously excluded from inventory were added and period manufacturing costs previously included were dropped. However, there was no material net change in the amount of the inventory. In other cases overhead rates had been unchanged for several years and revision to reflect increased costs of labor and other items gave rates for variable expense alone which were as high as the overhead rates previously used to cost production. Again, reclassification of costs was accomplished without material change in cost of inventory.

There were, however, a few companies which had introduced direct costing despite the fact that a change in cost of inventory was necessary. One of the following procedures was followed by these companies:

1. At the time direct costing was adopted, the year-end inventory was costed at direct cost and the period costs thereby eliminated were charged off. The change was made in a year when sales were high and closing inventory low in order to minimize the impact of the adjustment.

2. The period cost component of the closing inventory at the time of changeover was amortized over a period of years. In some cases, the period cost balance was extinguished by credits resulting from upward revisions of standard costs which accompanied rising prices of direct cost factors. A year when the closing inventory was low was chosen for the change.

3. Period costs in inventory at the time of changeover were transferred to a separate inventory account which has not been amortized. This account is combined with the current inventory (stated at direct cost) for reporting to stockholders. These companies expect to eliminate the period cost balance at some future time if problems attending the write-off can be solved.

From experience of companies participating in this study, it can be seen that in cases where inventories contain a substantial amount of period cost, the conversion to direct costing may have a serious impact on profits if the accumulated period cost is written off in the year of changeover. This impact can be reduced by practices such as making the change in a year when inventory is low or by spreading the write-off over a number of years.

Practice in Costing Inventory	
Direct cost	17
Full cost on absorption basis	24
Partial absorption basis	5
Prime cost	4
	50

Exhibit 16

As may be seen in Exhibit 16, 29 of the 50 companies continue to include period costs in inventory for purposes of external reporting. This requires procedures to adjust periodic inventory and income figures by adding or subtracting the change in period cost component of inventory. By utilizing such procedures, the advantages of direct costing are obtained for internal purposes without change in the method of costing inventories for external reports.

In most cases, the period cost component of inventory is carried in a separate account. The balance in this account is usually adjusted monthly or quarterly although, in cases where the amount and composition of the inventory varies little, adjustment may be made only at the year-end. Monthly or quarterly adjustments are usually made to avoid large adjustments to inventory and profit at the end of the year. One company's accounting manual explained its practice in the following words:

> "Corporate financial policy and year-end reporting requirements dictate an adjustment of the Overhead In Inventory account at December 31. Since it is not possible to predict the year-end inventory level and since a very large adjustment in December would cause an undesirable distortion of that period's profit, the practice is to adjust the account monthly. In effect, this is a conversion to absorption costing and admittedly negates one of the purposes of direct costing—that is, the gearing of profits to sales without the influence of production levels."

Comparatively simple procedures are employed to determine the amount of the periodic adjustment. The following examples illustrate practices reported by companies participating in the field study:

1. At the time this company began using direct costing, approximately two million dollars in period costs was separated from the inventory and charged to an account called "Deferred Overhead." At the end of each year, the amount to be carried in this account during the subsequent twelve months is determined as follows:

   If the year's output has been in excess of normal (i.e., 3,000,000 units), the period costs incurred during the year are divided by the actual production which gives the costing rate to be applied to the units on hand. Conversely, if the year's output had been less than 3,000,000 units, the rate is calculated as illustrated below:

   $$\frac{\text{Actual volume}}{\text{Normal volume}} \quad \frac{2,400,000}{3,000,000} = \text{Pct. of normal (80\%)}$$

Period expenses incurred during the year	$5,000,000
Deduct: Period expenses applicable to idle facilities	1,000,000
Period expenses applicable to production	$4,000,000

   The amount of period expense applicable to production ($4,000,000) is divided by the actual volume to obtain an overhead rate for charging the closing inventory with fixed expense.

94

$$\text{Costing rate} = \frac{\text{Period Expense Applicable to Production}}{\text{Actual volume}}$$

$$= \frac{\$4,000,000}{2,400,000 \text{ units}} = \$1.66\frac{2}{3}$$

Fixed expense applicable to idle facilities ($1,000,000) is charged off like underabsorbed overhead in absorption costing systems.

The calculations described above are made once a year solely for determining inventory and income figures for external financial reports including the income tax return.

2. Unlike the company in Example 1, this company manufactures a variety of products for which there is no common physical measuring unit. Therefore, period expense is expressed as a rate per dollar of direct labor and direct expense at normal volume.

The dollar amount of direct labor and direct expense in the year-end inventory is then multiplied by the foregoing rate to arrive at the period expense component of the closing inventory. These calculations may be summarized in the following formula:

$$\frac{\text{Period expense at normal volume budgeted for 1960}}{\substack{\text{Standard direct labor and} \\ \text{standard direct manufac-} \\ \text{turing expense at normal} \\ \text{volume budgeted for 1960}}} \times \substack{\text{Direct labor and direct manufac-} \\ \text{turing expense dollar content of} \\ \text{1959 closing inventory}}$$

Approximate adjustments are made monthly if needed to avoid a large year-end adjustment. The previous year's rate, modified by judgment if necessary, is applied to the current month's inventory of direct labor and direct expense.

Calculations described above, which include general company period expense, are made only for preparing consolidated statements. In this respect, the adjustment of inventory to absorption cost is similar to the application of LIFO which is likewise made only at the general company level.

3. A third company allocates all manufacturing overhead to production departments with the result that period manufacturing cost is collected in seven major pools corresponding to the company's major product lines. However, the period costs are not allocated to individual products within product lines. At the end of each month, period cost is transferred from inventory to cost of sales on the basis of relative amounts of direct cost in production and sales. Since the amount of period cost associated with the several product lines varies widely, it is thought desirable to make the segregation by product lines for external financial reporting purposes.

Unlike the preceding examples where the amount of period expense included in inventory is calculated statistically, in this company the actual period expense is allocated to product lines in the course of accounting for manufacturing cost.

Summary

In considering the question of acceptability of direct costing in preparing external financial reports, this chapter begins with the thesis that external financial reports should conform to standards which are accepted or required for the purpose. However, the principal statements of standards applying to inventory costing either leave the question without specific answer or reflect divided opinion. Moreover, opinions advanced in these statements are not supported by evidence or reasoning and hence they offer little guidance to the accountant who wishes to arrive at an independent opinion on the issue.

The present study shows that some companies using direct costing now cost inventories in external financial reports at direct cost and that many of the remaining companies expressed interest in bringing their external financial reports into conformity with internal accounting procedures. In most of these cases action has not been taken primarily because acceptance of direct costing for federal income tax purposes has not been obtainable, although there are also unresolved doubts with respect to acceptability of direct costing for public reporting. The study shows that comparatively simple adjustments suffice for restoring the applicable amount of period cost to inventory when external reports are prepared from accounts kept on a direct costing basis.

chapter 8

THE INCOME TAX STATUS
OF DIRECT COSTING

The principle to be followed with respect to inventories for federal income tax purposes is stated as follows by the Internal Revenue Code:[28]

> ". . . inventories shall be taken . . . on such basis as the Secretary or his delegate may prescribe as conforming as nearly as may be to the best accounting practice in the trade or business and as most clearly reflecting the income."

As defined by federal income tax regulations, inventory cost includes costs of (1) the raw materials and supplies which enter into or are consumed in connection with the manufacture of a product, (2) the direct labor expended thereon, and (3) the indirect expenses incident to and necessary for the production of the particular article, including in such indirect expenses a reasonable proportion of management expenses. Items (1) and (2) of the above definition seem clearly to identify direct material and direct labor, both of which are included in cost of inventory where direct costing is in use. On the other hand, the "indirect expense" component of inventory is broadly described and requires interpretation before the tax status of direct costing can be determined.

Interpretation of Law and Regulations by Courts

Court decisions might be expected to contain interpretations of law and regulations which would shed light on the acceptability of direct costing for determining taxable income. Three cases are often cited as relevant to the question. These are the Montreal Mining Co., Frank G. Wikstrom and Sons, and Geometric Stamping Co. cases.

(1) *Montreal Mining Co.* (2 T. C. 688, affirmed on this issue, C.C.A. 6, 1944, 33 A.F.T.R. 1660). In this case, the Commissioner of Internal Revenue disputed inclusion in inventory of various state and federal taxes (e.g., real and personal property, state income, franchise, social security, unemployment insurance) on grounds that they were not indirect expenses

---

[28] Internal Revenue Code of 1954, Sec. 471.

of production within the meaning of the tax regulation. The effect of excluding these expenses was to reduce "gross income from the property" and consequently to reduce the deduction for depletion. In upholding the Commissioner, the court commented as follows:

> "It is evident that the regulations do not expressly include taxes as an item of cost. None the less, the petitioner (Montreal Mining) claims that they are factors properly entering into the cost of inventory because (1) the practice conforms with the accounting method consistently followed by both the petitioner and a large part of the industry and (2) they are indirect expenses incident to and necessary for the production of ore. We do not agree that they are indirect expenses nor that they are proper items to include in inventory because of having been consistently treated this way."

Exclusion of expenses from inventory here was advantageous to the Commissioner. In the Wikstrom case, where exclusion was advantageous to the taxpayer, the Commissioner added similar expenses to inventory cost.

(2) *Frank G. Wikstrom & Sons, Inc.,* (20 T.C. No. 45, May 15, 1953.) The Commissioner here objected to including in inventory only direct labor and material attributable to specific contracts, with all other expenses being deducted from income in the year the expenses were incurred. This method had been consistently used by the taxpayer since incorporation. Wikstrom's inventory cost was recomputed by the Commissioner to include an allocated share of officers' salaries, rent, taxes, depreciation, repairs, light, heat, power, insurance, employees' welfare, factory stores, indirect factory labor, vacation, holiday, and bonus pay. The court held that the petitioner did not show that the Commissioner had exceeded his authority and hence the action of the Commissioner was upheld.

(3) *The Geometric Stamping Co.* (26 T.C. 301). Beginning in 1946, this company prepared its tax returns on a direct costing basis, although it continued to keep its books on an absorption costing basis. The Commissioner accepted the Company's use of direct costing in its tax returns for the years 1946 through 1948. For 1948, an overassessment of tax amounting to $11,757 was first determined, based on the theory that income should have been computed on an absorption basis rather than on a direct costing basis. However, this position was later reversed by the Commissioner and the Company received and accepted a much smaller refund which apparently related to other issues.

Subsequently when the Commissioner examined Geometric's tax returns for the years 1949-50 he found that taxable income had been understated by $13,368 by reason of failure to include certain indirect expenses in the inventory. This finding reversed the position taken in the previous years, possibly because the result was favorable to the government while in preceding years the taxpayer would have been entitled to a refund.

The Tax Court held that the Company's method of reporting for the tax years 1949-50 was proper on grounds that the taxpayer had consistently followed requirements laid down by the Commissioner. In this case the Commissioner did not contest the propriety of the direct costing method and the Court specifically excluded this question in the decision.

The Montreal Mining Co. and Geometric Stamping Co. cases are sometimes cited as offering support for direct costing. In the latter case, the company succeeded in changing to direct costing without requesting the Commissioner's permission in advance. However, neither of these cases provided a clear ruling on the acceptability of direct costing because the decisions were based on other issues. Thus the Court ruled for the taxpayer in the Geometric case because the Commissioner's regulations had been followed consistently by the taxpayer. In the case, the Commissioner did not question the propriety of direct costing as a method for determining inventory cost and the Court specifically excluded it from consideration.

After review of the cases described above, it seems necessary to conclude that the acceptability of direct costing for determining taxable income has not been decided by the courts.

Administrative Interpretations of Regulations

While a limited number of companies have formally requested the Commissioner's permission to change to direct costing, no statement of policy with respect to such requests has been issued. These requests have usually been either denied or unanswered, but informal permission has been granted in a few instances. Other companies have changed to direct costing without requesting permission. In some instances these changes have been challenged while in other instances no objections have been raised. There are also companies that have always used direct costing and the method has usually not been questioned in these cases. From this evidence, it seems apparent that cases have

99

been handled on an individual basis and decisions have not been uniform. However, the following observations can be made, based upon company experience reviewed in the course of this study:

1. Conversion to direct costing has been successfully accomplished when the change does not cause a material reduction in net income for the period of changeover. This requires special circumstances such as a low closing inventory or prior use of a cost classification plan which can be revised without making a material net change in inventory cost.

2. When the inventory contains a substantial amount of period cost, permission to write off this period cost in changing to direct costing has usually been denied. Some companies nevertheless changed to direct costing, but continue to carry in an asset account the amount of period cost in inventory at the time of changeover. However, in a few instances companies have received permission to write off the fixed component of the opening inventory over a period of years.

3. Where direct costing has been consistently used for a period of years, it usually has not been challenged. However, in a few instances the government has attempted to collect additional tax by demanding that a portion of the period cost be charged to inventory in a year when this would be to the government's advantage.

4. Requests for permission to change to direct costing have frequently been unanswered by the Commissioner of Internal Revenue. The effect has been, for the time being at least, equivalent to denial.

Where the amount of period cost currently included in inventory is material, it seems likely that the government will oppose any attempt to write-off this period cost because the government could sustain substantial losses in tax revenue. Moreover, uncertainty with respect to acceptability of direct costing as a method for determining taxable income carries the possibility that the method may be challenged at some future time when it is to the government's advantage to do so. For these reasons, a majority of the companies participating in this study continue to report income for tax purposes on an absorption costing basis. This is accomplished by relatively simple adjustments to inventory and cost of sales. Procedures for determining the amount of such adjustments were described in Chapter 7.

Comments Regarding Tax Status of Direct Costing

By analysis, it is possible to explore some of the consequences which could be expected to follow if direct costing were accepted for determining taxable income. These comments are derived solely from reasoning and they are not intended to reflect present administrative interpretation of the tax law nor to forecast future developments.

In view of the federal government's need for revenue, it can be expected that the Commissioner of Internal Revenue will oppose changes in accounting methods which would enable taxpayers to realize substantial tax savings. The write-off and deduction of period costs in inventory at the time direct costing is introduced would, in many cases, result in a material reduction of taxable income for the year. However, it would be possible for the Commissioner to permit taxpayers to change to direct costing and to report income on a direct costing basis in subsequent years without permitting the period cost component of the opening inventory in the year of changeover to be deducted. For tax purposes, this figure would simply remain in the balance sheet as a deferred cost which could not be deducted until liquidation of the inventory. In this respect, it would be analogous to a non-depreciable asset such as land, the cost of which cannot be deducted until the asset is disposed of. Under this procedure, the government would suffer no loss of revenue and the taxpayer would remain in the same position he would be in had he continued to use absorption costing. Under absorption costing the full amount of period cost can be deducted only when there is no closing inventory of manufactured goods. As an alternative, the impact on tax revenues could be spread by permitting systematic amortization over a period of years.

Direct costing will, however, provide a continuing tax advantage to a growing company which continues to increase its inventory of manufactured goods. If absorption costing is used under the same conditions, the amount of period cost deferred in inventory continues to increase so long as growth continues. Hence the amount of period cost deducted in determining taxable income will be less under absorption costing than it will under direct costing.

Exhibit 17 illustrates this difference. In the illustration, it is seen that the closing inventory increases each year for four years and that in each of these years net profit before tax as computed by absorption costing exceeds net profit before tax computed by direct costing. By the end of the fourth year, the cumulative difference in profit before tax has grown to $8,000. From the reconciliation schedule at the end of the exhibit, it can be seen that this is the cumulative amount of period cost deferred in

Illustration Showing Difference between Taxable Income under Absorption Costing and Direct Costing Assuming Continuing Growth

| | YEAR | | | | | |
	1	2	3	4	5	Totals
Production (units)	100,000	102,000	112,000	122,000	114,000	550,000
Sales (units)	90,000	100,000	110,000	120,000	130,000	550,000
Closing inventory (units)	10,000	12,000	14,000	16,000	-	-

Annual Income Statements Using Absorption Costing

	1	2	3	4	5	Totals
Sales	$90,000	$100,000	$110,000	$120,000	$130,000	
Cost of goods m'fgd*	90,000	91,800	100,800	109,800	102,600	
Add: Opening inventory	-	9,000	10,800	12,600	14,400	
Cost of goods available	90,000	100,800	111,600	122,400	117,000	
Less: Closing inventory	9,000	10,800	12,600	14,400	-	
Cost of goods sold	81,000	90,000	99,000	108,000	117,000	
Volume variance	-	(1,000)	(6,000)	(11,000)	(7,000)	
Total	81,000	89,000	93,000	97,000	110,000	
Profit before tax	9,000	11,000	17,000	23,000	20,000	80,000
Income tax (52%)	4,680	5,720	8,840	11,960	10,400	41,600
Profit after tax	4,320	5,280	8,160	11,040	9,600	38,400

*Standard production cost:

Direct $.40
Period ($50,000 per year, standard volume 100,000 units) .50
$.90

(In order to simplify the illustration, nonmanufacturing costs are omitted. Such costs would change the amount but not the trend of annual net profit figures.)

Exhibit 17

Annual Income Statements Using Direct Costing

	YEAR					Totals
	1	2	3	4	5	
Sales	$90,000	$100,000	$110,000	$120,000	$130,000	
Cost of goods mfg'd.	40,000	40,800	44,800	48,800	45,600	
Add: Opening inventory	-	4,000	4,800	5,600	6,400	
Cost of goods available	40,000	44,800	49,600	54,400	52,000	
Less: Closing inventory	4,000	4,800	5,600	6,400	-	
Cost of goods sold	36,000	40,000	44,000	48,000	52,000	
Marginal income	54,000	60,000	66,000	72,000	78,000	
Period costs	50,000	50,000	50,000	50,000	50,000	
Profit before tax	4,000	10,000	16,000	22,000	28,000	80,000
Income tax (52%)	2,080	5,200	8,320	11,440	14,560	41,600
Profit after tax	1,920	4,800	7,680	10,560	13,440	38,400

Reconciliation Between Absorption and Direct Costing Profit Figures

	1	2	3	4	5
Absorption costing, Profit before tax	$9,000	$11,000	$17,000	$23,000	$20,000
Change in inventory (units)	+ 10,000	+ 2,000	+ 2,000	+ 2,000	- 16,000
Change in amount of period cost in inventory	+$ 5,000	+$ 1,000	+$ 1,000	+$ 1,000	-$ 8,000
Direct costing profit before tax	$ 4,000	$10,000	$16,000	$22,000	$28,000

Exhibit 17—(Cont'd)

inventory under the absorption costing method, but charged against annual revenues under direct costing. In the fifth year it is assumed that the entire inventory is liquidated and the accumulated period cost is charged off. Over a complete cycle of inventory build up and liquidation both methods give the same cumulative profit. However, in a going concern complete liquidation of inventory would not occur and the opportunity to deduct the deferred period cost would be postponed indefinitely.

Once the changeover to direct costing has been effected, the timing of net income may differ from what it would have been under absorption costing, but year-to-year differences tend to offset over a series of years. Except for the continuing growth in inventory mentioned above, in the long run the same amount of taxable income will be reported regardless of which method is used[29].

While the fact that direct costing and absorption costing affect the timing of reported profits seems to be generally known, writers on the subject have not called attention to the fact that variations in the figure chosen for standard volume produce similar shifts in the timing of reported income under absorption costing alone. This is illustrated in Exhibit 18. In this exhibit, net profit has first been computed for a given set of facts using a manufacturing overhead rate based on a standard volume of 111,111 units per year. Profits are then recomputed, using the same facts with the exception that the manufacturing overhead rate is based upon a standard volume of 100,000 units per year. It can be seen that these different overhead rates cause different amounts of period cost to be deferred in inventory from year to year.

It can be reasoned but not proved that direct costing might produce a time pattern of income reporting and tax payments which would have certain advantages. In years when business activity is expanding, many companies increase inventories of manufactured goods. Where absorption costing is in use, this accumulation of inventory tends to increase reported profits in years when profits are already high because business is good. On the other hand, when business activity declines, production is cut back and inventories are reduced. This liquidation of period costs previously deferred in inventory tends to reduce reported profits still further in periods of recession. Thus, through its effect on the timing of profits, absorption costing may be a factor

---

[29] For explanation and illustration of these statements, see N.A.A. Research Series No. 23, Chapter 5.

Effect on Net Profit of Change in Standard Volume

Basic data: sales, production, unit variable cost, and annual fixed cost are taken from Exhibit 16. In the income statement below, unit manufacturing cost is based upon a standard volume of 111,111 units per year in contrast with 100,000 units per year used in Exhibit 16. The resulting unit cost is computed as follows.

Direct cost	$.40
Period cost ($50,000 per year ÷ 111,111 units)	.45
	$.85

Net Profit before Tax Based on Standard Volume of 111,111 Units Per Year

	YEAR 1	2	3	4	5	Totals
Sales	$90,000	$100,000	$110,000	$120,000	$130,000	$550,000
Cost of goods mfg'd.	85,000	86,700	95,200	103,700	96,900	
Add: Opening inventory	-	8,500	10,200	11,900	13,600	
Cost of goods available	85,000	95,200	105,400	115,600	110,500	
Less: Closing inventory	8,500	10,200	11,900	13,600	-	
Cost of goods sold	76,500	85,000	93,500	102,000	110,500	
Volume variance	5,000	4,100	(400)	(4,900)	(1,300)	
Profit before tax	8,500	10,900	16,900	22,900	20,800	80,000

Net Profit before Tax Based on Standard Volume of 100,000 Units Per Year

	YEAR 1	2	3	4	5	Totals
Net profit before tax (from Exhibit 16)	$ 9,000	$ 11,000	$ 17,000	$ 23,000	$ 20,000	$ 80,000
Difference	+$ 500	+$ 100	+$ 100	+$ 100	-$ 800	-

Exhibit 18

contributing toward the alternate periods of over optimism and over pessimism which seem to characterize the business cycle.

Under direct costing, accumulation or reduction of inventory has no effect on the amount of profit reported. For this reason, direct costing should have no tendency to accentuate cyclical swings in business psychology. At the same time it might tend to stabilize tax revenues over a period of years without reducing the total amount of tax collected.

It seems to be generally agreed that accounting practices required for tax purposes should not establish standards for other purposes, but that the relationship should run in the opposite direction. That is, what is accepted as good accounting practice for other purposes should have substantial weight in determining what practices are acceptable for determining taxable income. Recognition is given to this point of view in the income tax law by the statement that inventories are to be taken on a basis that conforms to best accounting practice and most clearly reflects income. As direct costing comes to be more widely used by industry, it seems reasonable to expect that it will also be accepted for tax purposes, particularly since it would probably not make a material difference in the amount of taxable income reported over a period of years.

Summary

After review of the principal relevant cases, this chapter concludes that court decisions do not provide a clear answer to the question of acceptability of direct costing for determining taxable income because the decisions have been based on issues other than direct costing. In administering provisions of the Internal Revenue Code relating to inventories, administrative decisions have not been uniform. In view of the uncertainty which prevails, most of the companies participating in this study adjust inventory to an absorption costing basis in determining income reported on tax returns.

The chapter concludes with comments based on analysis employed to explore the possible consequences which would ensue if direct costing were accepted for determining taxable income. This analysis first assumes that the government may be expected to oppose any accounting practice which would cause an important loss of tax revenue. For this reason, taxpayers who change to direct costing would probably be required to forego deduction of period costs already accumulated in the inventory.

Once conversion to direct costing has been effected, a company with a steadily growing inventory will continue to report a smaller net income under direct costing than under absorption costing. The reason is that absorption costing causes the amount of period cost deferred in inventory to increase. This period cost continues to be deferred until the inventory is liquidated without replacement. In a going company, indefinite postponement of the tax deduction results. For this reason, a growing company can be expected to pay somewhat lower income taxes under direct costing, but acceptance of direct costing for tax reporting would probably not result in a substantial tax loss to the government.

List of Companies Participating in This Study

The following companies were among those participating in this N.A.A. research study by contributing information regarding their methods. The remaining companies preferred that their names not be listed:

1. Adams-Millis Corporation
2. Aluminum Company of America
3. American Brake Shoe Company
4. American Can Company
5. American Enka Corporation
6. Armstrong Cork Company
7. Behr Manning Company
8. Berkline Corporation
9. Berkshire Knitting Mills
10. Bostitch, Inc.
11. Chicksan Company
12. Coats & Clark Inc.
13. Coast Manufacturing and Supply Co.
14. Dewey & Almy Chemical Division of W. R. Grace & Co.
15. Dixon Corporation
16. Fostoria Glass Company
17. Forstner, Inc.
18. Hancock Industries
19. A. S. Harrison Company
20. Johns-Manville Fiber Glass Inc.
21. Libby-Owens-Ford Glass Company
22. Neapco Products Inc.
23. North American Rayon Corp.
24. Ohio Rubber Company Division of Eagle-Picher Co.
25. Owens-Illinois Glass Co.
26. Chemical Specialties Division, Pennsalt Chemicals Corp.
27. Philco Corporation
28. Pioneer Manufacturing Co., Inc.
29. Sangamo Electric Company
30. San Juan Fishing & Packing Co.
31. Sperry Products, Inc.
32. Textile Machine Works
33. Union Metal Manufacturing Co.
34. Vanadium Corporation
35. Van Dorn Iron Works Co.
36. Vega Industries, Inc.
37. Weatherhead Company
38. Wheeling Stamping Company

N.A.A. ORGANIZATION FOR RESEARCH

N.A.A. research reports are presented in furtherance of the Association's educational objectives in the field of managerial accounting. These objectives are (1) to provide leadership in the continuing evolutionary development of managerial accounting, (2) to disseminate knowledge of managerial accounting techniques and their uses, and (3) to encourage wider adoption of the best practices.

Research projects are initiated by the Research Planning Committee, acting with approval of the National Board of Directors. The Research Staff collects information, analyzes this material, and prepares reports presenting findings. A Research Project Committee supplies guidance to the Staff in each study. When it is the consensus of the Committee that a research report merits consideration, publication is recommended.

Research Project Committee for Study
Current Application of Direct Costing

John V. James, *Chairman*
Dresser Industries, Inc.
Dallas, Texas

R. Lee Brummet
The University of Michigan
Ann Arbor, Michigan

C. G. Davison
Pittsburgh Plate Glass Co.
One Gateway Center
Pittsburgh, Pa.

M. O. Ehlert
Sangamo Electric Co.
Springfield, Illinois

R. N. Gifford
The Van Dorn Iron Works Co.
Cleveland, Ohio

F. D. Holford
Oscar Maver & Co.
Madison, Wisconsin

J. Grandel Jones
Bostitch, Inc.
East Greenwich, R. I.

T. H. Kerry
Aluminum Company of America
Pittsburgh, Pa.

Ray A. Longenecker
Armstrong Cork Co.
Lancaster, Pa.

J. P. McKenna
Hoffman-La Roche, Inc.
Nutley, N. J.

Samuel F. Mirandy
Lybrand, Ross Bros. & Montgomery
New York, N. Y.

R. W. Nopper
Johns-Manville Fiber Glass Co.
Toledo, Ohio

R. S. Overman
American Enka Corp.
Enka, N. C.

Lee G. Phillips
Lenkurt Electric Co., Inc.
San Carlos, Calif.

Richard K. Portman
Carton and Container Division
General Foods Corp.
Battle Creek, Michigan

Robert H. Sommer
Sylvania Electric Products, Inc.
New York, N. Y.

E. J. Swartz
The Union Metal Manufacturing Co.
Canton, Ohio

W. A. Thorn
The Berkline Corporation
Morristown, Tenn.

D. J. Wait
General Electric Co.
Schenectady, N. Y.

Robert B. Wetnight
Western Michigan University
Kalamazoo, Michigan

H. O. Williams
Adams-Millis Corp.
High Point, N. C.

W. R. Wright, Wright Associates, New York, N. Y.